SHARING OF SCRIPTURE

by

Clarence and Edith Roberts

Paulist Press

New York/Ramsey/Toronto

Library of Congress
Catalog Card Number: 78-61724

ISBN: 0-8091-2141-7

Published by Paulist Press
Editorial Office: 1865 Broadway, New York, N.Y. 10023
Business Office: 545 Island Road, Ramsey, N.J. 07446

Printed and bound in the
United States of America

Contents

Appendices

Preface

The Scripture study program we call "Sharing Scripture" (S.O.S.) was started in January, 1973, as an outgrowth of a dream and an increasing desire of Catholics to have a program of continuing education in Scripture.

We were at the right place at the right time and prepared with material that we had used since 1970 in a small study group in our own home. This group was made up of couples we knew in our area and at first we designed our own questions.

Then, thanks to the Spirit, and friends like Sr. Dorothy Donnelly, we were introduced to Father Edward Glynn, S.J. from the Jesuit School of Theology in Berkeley. With his help we completed twenty-five discussion lessons for the Book of Acts. Dody Donnelly urged us to keep those lessons and we did, for we were convinced by this time that we needed an ongoing Scripture study program for our fellow-parishoners.

However, for the next two years, despite our efforts nothing happened. Aside from our team, there was little interest in the project. But in June of 1972 while meeting with Father Ron Carignon, O.M.I., Coordinator of Adult-Ed for the Oakland Diocese. Scripture studies became the topic of the conversation. He suggested that we start our own course and his office would help wherever they could.

The first boost was a place for classes: an unused seminary near our home, possible site of an Adult Education Center for the diocese. With the help of Fr. Al Garrotto, O.M.I., we opened in January of 1973 with a revamped 13-week "Thematic Approach" to the Book of Acts.

At the same time Father Carignon introduced us to Marie Egolf, Adult Education Director of a neighboring parish. Marie was also interested in Scripture. Soon we found Fr. Michael Cook, S.J. and started our first evening class in Marie's parish.

Imagine our surprise that first January 10th when more than 100 people arrived for the two classes. We now have 15 centers in the Oakland Diocese with trained leaders, and have started seven more outside the diocese, including Soledad Prison, a maximum security facility.

Our Mini-Scripture lessons, in capsule form, also appeared every two months in a Bible Study column in *Catholic Charismatic* magazine, Paulist Press, 545 Island Road, Ramsey, N.J. 07446. (See Appendix.)

If we tried to mention the names of those who have helped us in putting this book together, the list would be too long, so many have been our helpers. To mention only a few:

> Dody Donnelly, C.S.J. who edited this book. Her persistent encouragement and prodding made us hang in there. Without her there would be *no* book.

Michael Cooke, S.J. who shared our dream and involvement from the start. He was the major contributor to Chapter III of this book.

The staff at Mt. Mary Immaculate.

The S.O.S. resource group.

The staff of Adult Ed, Diocese of Oakland under direction of Rev. Brian Joyce.

The typists whose many hours of work produced our final text: Jane Caccamo and Tony Gallegos.

Thanks to all!

The future of S.O.S. lies in the willingness of God's Spirit to use it as a tool to make us more aware of His action in the world and to draw us closer to Him. We hope that we'll keep in tune with the direction He is giving us.

It's been a source of great joy to watch people grow and develop their gifts through nourishing their hearts on God's Word. Who knows where we'll be led next?

Clarence and Edith Roberts
Martinez, California
September, 1978

Introduction

Holy Scripture, the inspired Word of God, is for many a sleeping giant. We feel that many want to awaken the giant and release its power to the multitude. It is past time for the Christian laity to use the long-dormant and precious tool of Scripture as a means of spiritual renewal and growth. To this end, we, the authors dedicate our God-given talents and energies. It was from this desire and dream that a program evolved called "Sharing of Scripture."

Sharing of Scripture started as a lay, non-profit organization operating primarily in the Oakland, California Diocese. But, as inquiries increased, it was introduced into the surrounding dioceses. Its success led to this book. We hope that this book, plus personal commitment and imagination, will help any group of people to start their own Sharing of Scripture program. So now—*What is Sharing of Scripture?* Sharing of Scripture is a program designed for those who are ready to start a more meaningful relationship with God through the study of Scripture. It is a progressive, ongoing (weekly throughout the school year) study designed but not limited to operate on a parish level.

The program is designed to work equally well with 10, 100, or more people. The emphasis is on sharing which is done in small groups under the direction of a trained leader.

Methodology

Before starting the Scripture study center, leaders must be trained and an organization set up. Our goal is a team effort acting with the Spirit at all times. Sharing of Scripture cannot be a one-man show.

> *To start an S.O.S. Center you need:*
> 1. A large meeting room to accommodate 50 or more.
> 2. Small areas that can be used for group discussions (5 or more).
> 3. Center Chairperson.
> 4. Discussion Leaders.
> 5. Commentator.
> 6. Greeters.
> 7. Participants.

Each participant receives one sheet of questions to be done as homework prior to the weekly meeting.

During the weekly meeting in small discussion groups led by a trained leader, each participant shares insights and answers to the questions.

Following the discussion session, each of the small groups assembles in one large group for a commentary on the passages that were studied during the week. This commentary should be held to 40 minutes. Allow sufficient time for questions from the floor.

This completes our session and participants pick up lessons for the following week on their way out.

Part 1

The First Step in Organizing
A Sharing of Scripture Program
For a Group or Parish

When you are ready to commit yourself to starting a Scripture study program, the first step is "publicity." Invite people in your local community who are interested in Scripture to come to an orientation, informational meeting. Choose whatever media is at your disposal for this communication; that is: local newspaper, local radio station, parish bulletin, etc.

An Outline of a
Typical Orientation Meeting:

Here begins the transcript of what we say to any group interested in starting a Scripture study center.

Scripture reading (Hebrews 4:12-13) or prayer:

> *For the Word of God is alive and active; it cuts more keenly than any two-edged sword piercing as far as the place where life and spirit, joints and marrow divide.*

It sifts the purpose and thoughts of the heart. There is nothing in creation that can hide from Him. Everything lies naked and exposed to the eyes of the great One with whom we have to reckon.

This passage seems to exemplify the challenge that Scripture has for us. We want to get to know ourselves better as God sees us. We know that we will not remain the same if we seriously and openly study the Scriptures. This course is for anyone who yearns to know more about God, Jesus, and the Church. It takes much discipline to direct ourselves in this manner, but the effort is ever so worthwhile. After all, all of us are changing whether we study Scripture or not.

The participants are told that if they study with an open mind and heart they can expect changes in their lives. They may or may not welcome these. What the changes will be and how they will come about remains for the individual and the Lord to work out.

Why choose Scripture for the tool of "Continuous Education"? Some feel that the changes in the Church came with such rapidity since Vatican II that a more stable support is needed. For others Scripture is so vital to learning about God's expectations, he/she speaks to us concerning our actions and attitudes throughout the readings. Scripture opens a whole new world and a new life.

Sharing of Scripture is an ongoing study. Spiritual growth is a continuing requirement if we and our communities are going to remain alive. To have a short course or introduction to Scripture with no plans or commitment to continue is like giving a person in the middle of a desert a sip of cool water, then turning and leaving him/her to start dehydrating all over again.

Our goal is to offer people an opportunity to grow and develop their gifts of the Spirit through entering into a closer relationship with Christ as we learn to know Him in Scripture.

Why are so many people afraid to study Scripture? Too many of us may suffer from having heard: "Don't bother reading the Bible; I'll tell you what it says!" And how did we get into such a position? To answer that question we have to go back to the time of the Reformation. When the Church split apart, Luther was emphasizing the Bible, and the Church was emphasizing the Sacraments. Protestants de-emphasized the Sacraments and Catholics de-emphasized the Bible. Everybody lost.

As the centuries rolled by some of the Church leaders began to recognize this but little was done about it. The Council of Baltimore in 1884 was the first to take any stand in the United States on the need for Scripture in the Church since the Reformation. And it was a rather weak stand in that it simply stated that each Catholic family should own and cherish a Bible. Nothing was mentioned about reading it, let alone studying it. It is only since the turn of the century that we see a renewed interest in the Bible expressed by Leo XIII establishing a commission for the promotion of Biblical studies and their protection from error. Pope Pius X gave it another boost but it took until the mid-1940's for Catholic scholars to start to emerge as recognized world authorities on Scripture.

However, very little of this had filtered down to the laity. By this time people were convinced that to read the Bible was not a good thing for fear of misinterpretation. It took Vatican II's statement encouraging the laity to read and *study* Scripture for any movement to start.

This movement for advancing the importance of Holy Scripture was slow because of the lack of encouragement from local church leaders who were themselves a product of a culture which did not encourage Scripture studies. But our Church today tells us that to renew our faith and to grow we must become spreaders of the Good News. This will come about only through study, knowledge, and inspiration of God's Spirit in Sacred Scripture.

So we have a choice: We can stagnate or grow spiritually. We've made some progress but we have a long way to go. And the road has to be traveled and experienced by all members of Christ's body. It may not be easy for some, but it is a responsibility that we need to take seriously. To prepare the way, we have developed a program which we think will help. We call it Sharing of Scripture.

Format for Sharing of Scripture

1. Each participant is given a sheet containing six to eight questions referring to the Scripture verses which are assigned for each lesson. Throughout the week each participant is asked to

read the Scripture passages, meditate on them, and answer each question prayerfully to seek out insights the Lord has for them. Writing these down is a good idea.

2. Once each week all participants assemble. The first week they are assigned to small groups. They remain in these for the whole course. In these small discussion groups, they share their answers to the questions given out the previous week. They also share ideas and insights that arose from Scripture reading.

3. After the sharing period (approximately 45 minutes) all of the sharing groups come together into one main body. The purpose of this general session is not to provide "right" answers for the questions that were discussed during the sharing period. It is rather to give a *different* dimension to the Scriptures. This is an exegesis to give an historical, cultural, and spiritual interpretation of the Scripture passages studied that week. We recommend this commentary to run approximately 30 – 40 minutes. We allow about 15 minutes at the end for questions from the group. These questions, at this time, could be generated from a response to what the commentator had to say. Or, they could include some questions which were not satisfactorily handled during the sharing session.

The Sharing of Scripture learning process is contrary to that to which some clergy have been exposed and therefore it usually brings up questions. We have selected this format because it allows more areas of freedom for the Spirit to move the heart. It provides a most welcome atmosphere for learning by encouraging an exchange of insights. This very often brings about a response from the most timid person who would otherwise never dare voice an idea. Fear of being wrong through not agreeing with the commentator inhibits many people.

The sharing *before* the commentator's remarks, then, is part of a sequence which we consider essential to the learning process. It also cleans the filters between God and His people so that God's message may come in with less static. This sequence allows the Spirit to work in our hearts enabling us to use our gifts and talents for the group. In Sharing of Scripture the exegetical input comes *last*!

The *question* has often been asked: Is the reason for having the commentator's remarks *last* so that the commentator can give us the right answers? To that we must answer, NO! NO! NO!

The reason is that we want the Spirit to be the primary teacher. The commentator's remarks are for additional input to be considered and for more depth and understanding of what God was saying to His people at the time that the manuscript was being created.

We believe that we need *three* exposures to Scripture in our S.O.S. program. First, the *liturgical* which most of us are familiar with in our churches. Second, the *prayerful* approach which we hope the questions inspire. Third, the *exegetical*, or scholarly approach which the commentator should supply. We feel that these three approaches are necessary for the good understanding of how God speaks to us:

1. **Through our own hearts.**
2. **Through our friends (others).**
3. **Through our liturgical community.**

After describing the format we handle questions from the floor. Then comes a request for commitment from those who would like to help start the program.

For the next four weeks, there will be leadership training one evening each week in preparation for the Scripture study. We found this to be essential because not only are leaders trained, but a community develops and the center operates on the "team effort" concept.

[[[[[

People frequently ask questions after the orientation talk, such as:
1. Can I come to the leadership training even if I don't think I'm ready to be a leader?
2. How much scriptural background do I need to be a leader?
3. What if I go through the training and become a leader and then fail?
4. What Bible do you recommend?

There are many more questions but we will address ourselves to these four since they have been asked at every orientation meeting we've ever had.

First, we do not ask for a commitment for leaders until the end of the training period of four weeks. All who are interested are invited to the training.

The discussion leader does not have to be a

Scripture scholar. No prior Scripture study is needed before starting with the rest of the group. The leaders will learn with their group and will not be required to answer any question which they do not feel comfortable answering. The leader is a facilitator, not an authority.

Then we have the fear of failure. We encourage everyone to try. Generally after the training, individuals will know if they can handle a small group. If one feels uncomfortable in the role but would really like to try, there is always the alternate-leader role or greeter.

What Bible to recommend? At the top of the list we would recommend the Oxford Study Edition of the New English Bible with the Apocrypha. The Jerusalem, and the New American Bible are also very good. There are many other modern translations of the Bible and study Bibles available today that are also useful. For the less expensive editions, use the Good News Bible in paperback.

After answering the questions from the group we make two assumptions before we continue. First, we assume that we have a group of people who would like to come together regularly to share and study Scripture.

Second, we assume that in this group there are a number of people who will commit themselves to participate in the leadership-training course. This does not necessarily mean that they must at this time make a commitment to *be* a leader. That comes later. The orientation meeting is ended and we are now ready to start the next phase of organizing a Sharing of Scripture group: Training small-discussion group leaders.

Training Small Group Discussion Leaders for Scripture Sharing

Leadership Training Outline In Four Sessions

A. Session One—Part One
   1. Introduction: Discuss Goals
   2. Leaders: Discussion—"Leadership"
   3. Self: Discussion—"Uniqueness"
   4. Qualities of a Leader
B. Session One—Part Two
   1. Exercise
   2. Evaluation
C. Session Two—Part One: "Communication"
   1. Review Session One
   2. Need for Communication
   3. Mechanics of Communication
   4. Communication Quality
   5. Communications Barriers
D. Session Two—Part Two
   1. Exercise
   2. Evaluation
E. Session Three—Part One: "The Small-Group Leader"
   1. Review

2. Common fears of small groups
F. Session Three—Part Two
   1. Exercise
G. Session Four—Part One: "Organization"
   1. Review
   2. Introduce Commentator
H. Session Four—Part Two: "Choosing a Center Chairperson"
   1. Duties of the Center Chairperson
   2. Assignment of Leadership
      a. Discussion Leaders
      b. Alternate-Leaders
      c. Greeters
      d. Registration Team

Remember: Group participation is very important throughout the workshop. Blackboards are desirable for jotting down words, outlines, comments and general "chalk-talk."

A. Session One—Part One

1. Introduction: Discuss Goals

Our purpose or goal in these next four sessions will be to develop small-group discussion leaders for our oncoming Scripture study program. It was pointed out to me that to start out with a statement which emphasizes our purpose as "the training of leaders" scares some people. This may be true; however, we think that people deserve honesty when they start a program. There is no commitment required at the start of the sessions. We ask only that those people who are interested in helping to start a Scripture study group attend the training sessions. Then we ask them to defer their decision about leading a small discussion group until the last session.

The rest of this chapter will discuss what we do to train people for our Sharing of Scripture parish-center or group. Our approach is something like this:

You do not have to be an expert on Scripture to lead a group. As a matter of fact, you do not need to have ever studied Scripture to be an effective leader in our program. You do need:

    a. The desire to grow spiritually.
    b. The desire to want others to grow spiritually.
    c. The desire to want to help others grow spiritually.

If you have these qualities, the Lord will help you with the rest—as we soon discovered from our own experience.

2. Leaders: Discussion—"Leadership"

Many people believe that:

    a. They are not leader material.
    b. Leaders are "born leaders" or they are not effective leaders.

This concept must be dealt with. It must be pointed out that each person has leadership qualities which can be developed. Sometimes it is difficult for a person who believes that leaders are "born" to accept the idea that leaders can be developed.

How to sell them on the idea? Just ask the group to name any leader they can think of. List the names on a blackboard. If a blackboard is not available simply list them on a piece of paper. The group usually names people like: the president, the pope, or Jesus. If they do this, ask about leaders in their community. Who are some of the community leaders? List them.

What about our homes? Who are the leaders there? List them.

Now together inspect the list. Is there anyone on that list who simply became a leader without some kind of training?

After a short discussion about how someone became a leader, we usually arrive at a point where it is mutually agreed that leaders must be developed, and taking it one step further, each person in the room has some leadership qualities. So each person possesses potential leadership though of course in varying degrees. But we are encouraged to develop our potential to the fullest. This includes our leadership abilities.

Let's consider what a leader is:

Ask the group what they think a leader is. You write their ideas on the blackboard. Some thoughts from a previous group are listed below:

    a. A leader is one who leads.
    b. A facilitator or moderator.
    c. One who sets an example.
    d. A supervisor or boss.
    e. An organizer.
    f. Someone who listens and cares, etc.

A leader is all of the above and more. We like the following definition: **A leader is a person who gets the groups to become aware of and to use their**

spiritual potential, to help others share of themselves. And sharing is part of the name of our program: "Sharing of Scripture." Our purpose or goal as a group leader is the spiritual growth of our **group**. In the sharing we put ourselves last.

In this, time is one of the most valuable single elements that we have. It isn't a physical element necessarily, but our ability to sacrifice **our** time so that others might grow may make the difference between people hearing what **we** say or allowing someone in our group to take even a small step toward understanding and getting closer to Christ.

Another way of looking at it is, the more work you can get your group to do, the less you have to do: awareness of the needs of others. It gets heavy. Let's backtrack a little and talk about "self."

3. Self: Discussion—"Uniqueness"

Before we can start leading other people, we must know first where *we* are. Let's talk about some of the things that we know. What do we know about ourselves?

Here, try to get the group to share some of the things they know about themselves. List them. If you get no immediate response from the group, start listing some of things you know about yourself.

I know that:
  a. I'm a man/woman.
  b. I like sailing.
  c. I enjoy the mountains, etc.

After exhausting either the space on the board or the feedback from the group, examine the list together.

So we find that people are *different*. All of us are unique, different persons. However, we do have some things in common. What are some of the things we have in common? (At this point the group usually names several things that people have in common.) List them on the blackboard.

One of, if not the most important thing we all have in common is that each of us has tremendous *needs*:

   a. Physical needs.
   b. Need for security.
   c. Emotional needs.
      1. Need to be loved.
      2. Need to love.
   d. Spiritual needs.
   e. Need to have communication with others.

I know that I have all of these needs and many more. So? *Good!* If I have all of these needs, then other people must have them also. What does this have to do with leading a small group? Try to get the group to react and respond to the question before summarizing. (We start preparing to lead a small group by developing an awareness or sensitivity to the others in the group.)

We are all unique individuals, God creates only originals.

Chalk talk:

Question: Why are we different? What makes us different? Exploit the group's ideas thoroughly before summarizing. While summarizing fit each of the elements from the group into their CE[4] (See-

Level), Dody Donnelly's mnemonic device for "Individual Background." (See "TEAM" by Dody Donnelly. Paulist Press, 1865 Broadway, N.Y. 10023.)

CE^4 Culture
         Environment
         Education
         Experience
         Expectation

> Extract the first
> letter of each
> word and it
> comes out
> *CEEEE-Level = See-Level*

I have my own individual see-level because no one has had the same exact Experiences, Education, Environment, or has the same Expectations. And, if I am different from everyone else, so is everyone here different from everyone else also.

So, in a small-group situation, your thoughts will be different. Isn't that great? Think of the amount of learning that you can do in a group of seven people when you as a member allow the other six to be considered. And, as a small-group leader, one of your responsibilities is to promote and allow the others' ideas to be heard and understood.

Let's turn to the individual again—*me*! I am different because I have an individual see-level. Because of this see-level I have a certain *value system* which determines what my attitudes are, which in turn determine what *action* I take.

Chalk talk:

> See-Level (CE^4) – Way to See
> Value System
> Attitudes (Habits)
> Action

Why is this so important? What does it mean?
Call upon the group to share ideas.

Summarize:

If you want to motivate a group into action their
attitudes must be favorable to your cause. If the
attitudes are not favorable you may not get the
results that you are trying to achieve. How do you
change attitudes of people?

You don't know? —
Of course you do! Their attitudes are determined
by their value system. So, we must change their
value system. How? By changing their see-level.
You want to get people to change? Change their
see-level. This you can do by changing any of the
"E's." Each of you is now engaged in changing
his/her see-level. Every encounter with another
person, every exchange of ideas, changes us
slightly. If this is true, then, we are constantly
changing.

But as a unique individual capable of free
choices we can do much to guide the direction
which we take. I have heard many people say, "Oh
I'd like to be a group leader, but I can't." If you
think you will fail as a group leader or as anything
for that matter, you will.

If, on the other hand, you think "success," you will have a certain measure of success even if it isn't 100%. For people who have a poor self-image, the first major step is to start working on that. If I am going to do well, I must think well of myself. There are many good books that can be very helpful. One which I particularly like is "Psychocybernetics" by Dr. Maxwell Maltz.

4. Qualities of a Leader

What are some qualities which you would like to see in a leader? Draw comments and qualities from the group. List them on the blackboard.

One of the most important assets of the small group leader is his or her ability to listen. Studies have been made by major universities during the past decade and a half and some interesting things have come out of these studies. For example, the talents that we use the least in life are the ones which we have spent the greatest time in training.

Of the time we spend communicating in one form or another we spend about twice as much reading as we do writing, twice as much speaking as we do reading, and one and a half times as much listening as we do speaking. So we spend the largest percentage of our communication time *listening*. As a result many major universities now have courses on "listening." It's only scratching the surface though, because most of us have had no training in this one thing which we're expected to do most of the time.

Another thing that was discovered by recent studies was that people without listening-training were operating at about 25% efficiency on a 10-minute talk. (Efficiency in terms of retention.) And as the time of the talk increased, the efficiency decreased. How many 10-minute lectures have you attended lately? After that question what else can we do but stop talking? Let's do an exercise.

B. Session One—Part Two of Leadership Training

1. An Exercise in Listening: "Mini-Lab"

Divide the group into small groups of eight or any convenient *even* number of persons. Divide each small group into two parts: A and B. Ask part A to form a group circle for discussion as shown in the diagram. Ask part B to pick a person in part A to observe. Each person in part B has a different person in part A to observe.

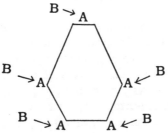

The object is to assign the inner group a topic for discussion. The inner group will discuss the topic and completely ignore the outer group. The outer group will listen to the inner group and at the given time when the discussion is over will give feedback to the person he/she was observing. The feedback will consist of what he/she heard the person say and how he/she thought the person felt on the issue.

Suggested Topics:
    a. How important is the expression of affection?
    b. Do people approach love in different ways?
    c. What do you think about religion?
    d. God?
    e. Praying together?
    f. Life after death?

The inner group has 10 to 15 minutes to select and discuss a topic. After that, time is called and the dyads go off together. After about five minutes everyone returns and the inner groups become the outer groups. The outers become inners and the same exercise is repeated. When the exercise is completed, the entire exercise is evaluated by everyone in the form of group sharing.

2. Evaluating the Exercise and the Evening

Lead questions which might encourage discussion are:

   a. What did you feel like as a member of the inner group?
   b. As an outer how did you feel when you couldn't talk?

C. Session Two—Part One: "Communication"

1. Review important parts of Session One
    a. Definition of leader.
    b. Concept of see-level.

2. Need for Communication

If we were to single out the most common problem we have in the world, our country, state, community, in our business world, or our family, it would be lack of communication. So communication or lack of it is probably the cause of most of the problems that we face in the world today.

That is a pretty big statement, so what about something a little closer to home? Ask the group if anyone cares to share a problem which they have had with another member of their family or a friend, not caused by lack of communication. If anyone thinks they have such a problem, explore it to determine the cause.

3. Mechanics of Communication

To have communication of any kind certain things are necessary. The person who has an idea that he/she wants to share with another person must transmit that idea through some media. The other person must be receptive to the idea and must understand it. And to make the communication complete the sender must have some feedback in order to know that his/her idea was received and understood. The essentials of communication then are:

    a. Sender.
    b. Receiver.
    c. Understanding.
    d. Feedback.

The idea can be transmitted in verbal form through such media as:

    a. Written word.

b. Television.

c. Radio.

d. Movies.

e. Telephone.

f. In person or face to face.

The sender may also transmit much of his/her ideas through non-verbal means. A great deal of today's communication is non-verbal. The tone of voice, perhaps the silence, or the body, or maybe just the look in the eyes, a kick under the table, or a slight nudge with the elbow. A kiss, how much can a kiss communicate to you? How little? All of these things have a way of communicating an idea and must be considered.

4. Communication Quality

Take an average day in your life. Examine it for your communication-quality. In the morning, do you greet anyone as you get up? How? When I awake, I seem to have the need to communicate the fact that I am awake and alive. This can take the form of anything from a grunt or yawn to some plot like getting one of my great danes to give my wife Edith a good morning kiss. And I usually get some feedback telling me that the message was received and understood.

Many people go through a normal day with relatively poor communication-quality. By communication-quality I mean the character or the value of the communication. The communication can be a nothing or it can be rich with dialogue nourishing the two people involved. An example of this is: As I arrive at work in the morning, someone I know is coming toward me:

"Good morning, how are you?" "Fine, how are -
- - - - -." It's a natural reaction which I have when
passing someone I know. I have been conditioned
to greet people in the morning or when I meet
them for the first time that day to ask them how
they are. I don't care how the person really feels
generally. The fact that the person is at work
means he/she must feel fairly well or he/she
wouldn't be there in the first place. Sometimes by
the time I hear "Fine! How are you?" I'm halfway
down the hall and we are separated by about 30 to
40 feet, and heading in opposite directions. It's
like a group of people alone and remaining
isolated though together because they have
revealed nothing of who they are.

As we progress in our look at the quality of our
communication, we take the next example:

I arrive at work at the same time another
person does. We are going in the same direction.
We have nothing to say to each other so we
exchange superficial greetings and discuss the
weather or simple news-facts that do not involve
either of us. I share none of my own thoughts
and I am not interested in the thoughts of the
other person. We could say we are hiding behind
general facts. You will find many examples of
this quality of communication at cocktail
parties, PTA meetings, lunch-room talk, and
sometimes even at home.

And then we have the next step in our ladder of
improving the quality of our communication.
Here I am willing to reveal a few of my ideas and
thoughts. I am still not interested in what you're
thinking or your ideas. The best way to become

aware of this quality of communication is to listen at conference breaks or meetings where there are two distinct thoughts being stated by two people appearing to be in conversation with each other.

I am now at a point where I am willing to reveal a little about myself, but the other person must listen and not interrupt with his ideas and thoughts, because I won't listen to them anyway.

As we climb higher in assessing the quality of our communication we take a look at another example. Here I can begin to tell you what I feel. I can disagree vehemently with your ideas and decisions but when I expose some of the feelings of fear, anxiety, and frustration that you also feel, then you begin to understand how I made this decision or had this idea and you begin to share some of your fears and frustrations with me. There is an exchange by two human beings who have the same feelings but may act them out differently.

The final step in the quality of communication is "peak experience" in which I share everything about myself with another person and he/she shares everything about himself/herself with me. This happens very rarely, if ever, in one's life. I can think of a couple of times when it has happened in my life and I wasn't able to remain in that environment. I had to move out of it because I was too vulnerable.

5. Communication Barriers

Chalk talk:

Draw from the group what they think are some of

the barriers to communication and list on the board:

   a. Not listening.
   b. Not having same definitions for same word.
   c. Interruptions.
   d. Emotional feeling, etc.

Let's discuss a few barriers. One that I consider major is evaluating and judging.

Example: When emotions are running high on a given topic, if I were to say to a group of people, "What's all this talk about the Church not being relevant to the world today? I think the Church speaks to all people in all facets of life today," the immediate reaction would probably be agreement or disagreement. Some would think: "He's absolutely right!" Others would think: "He's out of his mind!"

From that point on there would be very little active listening because an evaluation has been made and no one is really interested in *why* I feel the way I do. Any listening that takes place is in the form of a rebuttal instead of listening for understanding. Because to listen for understanding could be too dangerous.

So the first requirement for overcoming this barrier is courage and this I do not always have. We must risk listening to the other person's point of view if we are going to understand it. This is for me the most difficult thing to do because I must try to walk in the other person's moccasins. I could make a start by asking myself: What makes this guy tick? Why does he feel the way he does?

The next question would be why he/she said what he/she said.

Other barriers are:
   a. Criticizing the speaker's style
   b. Listening for facts instead of ideas
   c. Over-stimulation in the manner of speech; using loaded words
   d. Faking attention to the speaker
   e. Not telling it the way it is, rather telling it the way I'd like it to be

Now that we have identified some of the communication barriers, what can we do about them? Can we remove them? Of course we can, but it is usually not easy. And the hardest thing of all is to become aware that they even exist. Once we recognize that there *is* a barrier, removing it isn't all that hard.

For example, when I become aware that I'm criticizing the speaker's style or find him uninteresting I can ask myself, what does he know that I don't, or what does he have that I can use?

Finding myself faking attention and correcting that tendency is something which I have to work on continuously. I suppose it's because the average speaker speaks at the rate of 175 words per minute and the average person can think five times that fast. So I listen for 10 seconds and think of something else for 20 seconds, then back for eight seconds and out for 30 seconds, so - - - let's do an exercise.

(For a more extended approach to "Communication" see "TEAM" by Dody Donnelly.)

D. Session Two—Part Two:

1. Exercise

Form small groups of not more than eight people. This is a two-part exercise.

1st—Each person shares whatever he/she cares to about himself/herself with the group. Allow about two minutes for each person, then another couple of minutes to clarify any question that a group member may have about another. This can be strictly history, likes and dislikes, or a combination of both.

2nd—Each person tells every individual in the group two positive (nice) things about that person from what he/she has learned, perceived, or already knew about them—until everyone has shared with each person in the group.

2. Evaluation

Discuss with the whole group the quality of communication during this exercise. Compare with the exercise on listening. Was it difficult or easy to find two positive things to say about each person? We seem to be indicating at times, "I know there are lots of good things about you but I can't verbalize them."

Or, now and then we find a person who cannot risk being that personal with a single person and will speak on how great the dedication of people coming out for this is, how impressed he or she is. A session of this type usually breaks down barriers which would take several meetings to break down and the group can go about the thing they came for much sooner. The purpose of such an

exercise is to break through the usual little barriers which people put up that tend to keep
community from happening.

E. Session Three—Part One: "The Small Group Leader"

1. Review

Goals: define.

Self: needs, self-image, the key to success, see-
level.

Leader: define.

Communication: need for, mechanics, verbal,
nonverbal.

Barriers.

2. Common Fears of Small Groups

Chalk talk:

What are some common fears of small groups?
Make a list on the blackboard as the group calls
them out. If the group is slow in starting, encourage
them by asking them about some things they'd fear
when they join a small group . . . and it starts:

Fear of not knowing what it's about.

Fear of being known.

Fear of being ridiculed or sounding stupid.

Fear of being unqualified.

What is it going to cost me?

Fear of disappointment.

Fear of failure.

So we wind up with a list on the board. Is there
anyone here who when going into a small group

for the first time does not have some of these fears? What shall we do with all these fears? Get rid of them? Or try? How?

We may start by stating that no one will be required to do or say anything that he or she does not want to. Explain to the group that if we are to work as a group we will have to develop trust in each other and that trust implies that whatever is said in confidence in the group remains there. While discussing each of the fears with the group each member begins to see that others have similar fears and they begin to support each other. So it begins. . . .

F. Session Three—Part Two: Exercise: "How to lead small groups"

1. Introduction

This exercise is one in which you as prospective group leaders practice and critique your skills. The first question that usually comes up is, "What if I'm asked something I don't know?" As a small group leader of S.O.S. you are not expected to be an authority on Scripture. Nor are you required to answer questions except those that pertain to the format of the evening. As a small-group leader your first responsibility is to get the group to *share*. You can look upon questions directed to you as an opportunity to develop discussion. When asked a question you cannot answer, you might try this approach: Look around the group and make the observation: "That's a good question. Would anyone care to comment on it?" Give them a moment to think about it. Don't be afraid of silence. Put your trust in the group. They will usually come through. And if at first they don't respond, *don't* panic by attempting an answer even if you think you know it.

Try rephrasing the question and ask the group again. Remember *your* function is to make this group a *successful* discussion group. Sometimes it may be necessary to rephrase the question several times in order to get all the meat out of it. Then some prospective group leaders ask: **"Don't I get to share any of my answers too?"** Of course you do. That can take place in two ways:

a. The group leaders meet with the commentator before the regular session and share among themselves. At this point the commentator can also give a little input.

b. During the regular session the group leaders may share after they have encouraged each of the group members to share. If all points were covered, you may simply state: **"We've covered that pretty thoroughly; let's move on to the next question."**

Each small group should have a maximum of eight people, plus one person who has had experience in leading small groups. This person is there to clarify instructions if necessary and to observe the leaders. The group is to be made aware of the extra person and be told that the observer is not going to participate in the discussion. Each prospective leader in the group is allowed about ten minutes to lead the group, then about two minutes for critique. The prospective leader is rated on:

a. Did the group stay on the subject?

b. Did the leader come across as an authority figure?
c. Did the leader attempt to answer each question posed to him/her or was the group encouraged to share ideas on any question that was asked?
d. Did the leader help make the group successful?
e. Did the group work as a team?
f. Was the leader in a position to be aware of and to see the reactions of the group?

The person critiquing points out not only the areas that need improvement, but also those that were well done. The critique must be to the point so that the next leader may start within the timeframe available. A possible list of discussion topics follows:
a. Sample lessons from S.O.S.
b. Discussion of any of the topics which have been presented during the workshop such as:
   1. Self.
   2. Leaders.
   3. Communication.
   4. Communication barriers.
   5. Common fears of small groups.

G. Session Four—Part One: "Organization"

1. Review

This time (approximately 20 minutes) should be used as an opportunity to answer last minute questions people usually ask. The questions can be used as your basis of review to make certain that the important areas of the workshop were clearly understood.

2. Introduce the Commentator

This presupposes that the program of study has been selected. The commentator then gives a very brief breakdown of their approach in presenting the topic.

H. Session Four—Part Two: "Choosing a Center Chairperson"

1. The Center Chairperson's Duties Are As Follows:

    a. Presides over leaders' meetings.

    b. Leads the opening at each weekly meeting.

    c. Is generally responsible for announcements, getting lesson plans to leaders.

    d. Assigns leaders to their prospective groups and directs the registration of participants during the first meeting of S.O.S.

    e. Coordinates with the commentators.

    f. Generally deals with miscellaneous details as they occur, either directly or indirectly.

    g. In the Oakland Diocese, the center-chairperson is also a member of the executive board of S.O.S., representing the area and people they lead.

    h. Assures that leaders are part of the team by including them in all major decisions that involve the operation of the center.

2. Assignment of Leadership

At this time a commitment is asked of those who would like to be small-group discussion leaders. Some people are hesitant and would like to start out as alternate-leaders. This is good. Alternate-leaders are needed; however, if everyone signs up for alternate-leader then, automatically all alternates become regulars. Both commitments are encouraged. If your goals are establishing an over-all sharing-group of about fifty people, you need a minimum of five regular leaders and two alternates who fill in when one of the regulars cannot attend.

Arrange for members of your leadership team to arrive before the scheduled meeting and greet the general participants as they enter. It is very important that participants be welcomed as they arrive, particularly if it is their first time.

The registration team is only required at the first meeting so this can be done by the leaders or alternate-leaders.

Commentator

1. Qualifications

A. Must have the desire to want to help others to share in the discovery of Jesus Christ through the Scriptures.

B. Must be willing to work as a team member and with the center-chairperson within the basic concepts of the S.O.S. program.

2. Role

The structure of S.O.S. is such that the commentator **follows** the group discussions. From the point of view of the commentator, this has several advantages. The people have already read and prayed over the text privately in the light of the questions. They have discussed the text with their peers. Thus, they have already dealt with the text on the level of what does this say to me personally. Moreover, they have a good familiarity with the text before the commentator even begins to speak. They are ready to hear the text on another level.

Hence, the role of commentator is to bring to the people something that they most likely cannot do for themselves (for whatever reason, e.g., lack of time, resources, background, etc.). This is a level of expertise (which, of course, will vary from commentator to commentator) that can open up for the people a more technical and sophisticated reading of the Scriptures in the light of modern scholarship. This is extremely important, for people often hear about this or that "new" thing the Scripture scholars are saying but they have no first-hand experience of the kind of thinking that makes such developments possible. The commentator can afford a kind of concrete practicum of contemporary approaches. This may sound a bit "heady" (and indeed, it could get too academic), but a more serious mistake would be to talk down to the group. People today are entitled—and individuals need and want—to know what is going on in modern approaches to the Bible. They may not understand all the arguments in detail but at least they can get a "feel" for the type of argumentation used. It has been our experience that they are most appreciative of such input.

To be more concrete, the framework out of which the commentator speaks is one that recognizes the text (e.g., the Gospel of Matthew) as a literary creation written in a particular socio-cultural situation with a particular audience in mind. Matthew is certainly a confession of faith and this dimension is not ignored. Indeed, it is emphasized. But the approach continually poses the question: What is the author of Matthew trying to say? This involves questions such as, the structure of the Gospel, comparative literary phenomena (e.g., the Gospel of Mark), the world of the author, and most importantly the religious truth as distinct from the historical facts that the author is trying to communicate. Perhaps the most important and difficult task of the commentator is to overcome the 19th-20th century heresy: "If it didn't happen, it isn't true!"

Such an approach will obviously lead to a conflict for the people involved who have just worked out their own interpretation of the experience and now hear what seems like a totally different interpretation from the commentator. This is a healthy conflict and will be a growing experience for those who are open to it. At this point, the commentator must be sympathetic, truly hearing what the problem is, and yet firm. He or she should point out that there are different levels of reading Scripture, just as there are different levels of reading a novel: For pure enjoyment, because it speaks to some existential need in one's personal life, or as a literary critic. One doesn't have to be a literary critic to read a novel and one doesn't have to be a biblical scholar to read Scripture. One can get a great deal at any level but should always be open to further growth and development. The function of the commentator is to facilitate the growth to new levels.

3. Some Practical Points

A. It is helpful if the commentator meets for about a half hour with the leaders of the groups before the discussions, **not** to give a lecture, but simply to answer questions so as to facilitate the discussions.

B. The commentator should **not** participate in the group discussions. The tendency is for the group to defer to his/her expertise, which destroys the discussions.

C. The commentator's time should not be used for prayer, singing, announcements, etc. These are all things the people can do for themselves. He or she has something to bring to them that they cannot do for themselves and should protect the time allotted for that.

D. Emphasize: The only stupid question is the one that is not asked. The commentator must create an atmosphere of openness to questions that particularly obviates the fear of asking dumb questions. The more expertise the commentator has, the more necessary this will be.

E. The commentator should prepare a 30-40 minute exegesis of the text, using the best modern biblical scholarship available. He or she does not have to be a professional exegete, but must be aware of such modern biblical tools as the *Jerome Biblical Commentary* (Prentice-Hall), the *Old Testament and New Testament Reading Guides* (Liturgical Press), the various commentaries on individual books, such as the *Anchor Bible* series (Doubleday) or the commentaries put out by Pelican. There are also notes and tapes available through S.O.S. Each commentator will find some things more helpful than others, but should at least have enough resources to bring that dimension to the people which they cannot easily do for themselves. Also important are "The Cambridge Bible Commentary on the New English Bible" and the "Tyndale" Commentaries.

4

The Resource Groups

Scripture Resource People are groups that meet for the sole purpose of generating questions for the program lessons. These groups generally represent a wide variety of scriptural expertise. Previous scriptural study is not the main consideration. The ability to work as a team, love of Scripture, and the ability to formulate real questions are the three basic requirements for persons in a resource group. A wide variety of backgrounds is desirable thus enriching the overall flavor of the questions.

Our goal is to generate questions that will whet the appetite of beginning through advanced students. So then each lesson will have something special for each participant.

Each group functions with a leader who facilitates the meetings and assigns each member his/her material for the following week.

During a recent resource meeting, the group had the following assignments: Member #1—John 6:1-15; member #2—John 6:16-21; member #3—John 6:22-24; member #4—John 6:25-34; member #5—John 6:35-50; member #6—John 6:51-59; member #7—John 6:60-71; member #8—John 7:1-13; member #9—John 7:14-36; member #10—John 7:37-52.

Each member is asked to read his or her assignment, meditate on it, read available commentaries on it, then generate two questions having to do with the passage. The questions are brought before the group and are discussed, reworded, etc., as a group effort. Unless the person has two very outstanding questions, only one is retained. The group decides which one. In the assignment example just given, member #1's assignment completed questions for lesson No. 4. The assignments of members 2 through 7 constituted lesson No. 5. Members 8 through 10 gave us three questions for lesson No. 6, etc.

After the questions are introduced, discussed, and accepted by the group, they're collected by a member of the group who acts as a secretary. The questions are then typed into a lesson. Copies are made so that during the following week each member gets a copy and the questions are again scrutinized. They are not considered ready until they have been accepted a second time by the group.

Our resource group meets each week for one hour and a half. During that time old material is reviewed, new material introduced and assignments are given out. We have no goal as to the amount of material which we need to cover each time. We take ample time with each question and when we can no longer contribute more to the question we ask for a vote: "Accept or Reject," and we move on. At the end of the time allowed we stop and pick the matter up the following week. Briefly, that's how a resource group of Scripture-loving people prepare the lessons. However, if you'd rather study the Scriptures using S.O.S. material, this booklet makes lessons available so that you can get started. Additional lessons are available by request from S.O.S., 5558 Likins Avenue, Martinez, Ca. 94553.

Part 2

QUESTIONS FOR THE WEEKLY
LESSONS
FOR HOME MEDITATION AND
PRAYER
TO BE DISCUSSED AND
SHARED IN GROUPS EACH
WEEK

1

Book Of Acts

Lesson 1: Ascension

1. What earlier work is referred to by the author in Acts 1:1? How does Jesus' last instructions to the apostles seem to indicate this book is a completion of the first?

2. What do you find important about the apostles' questions to Jesus in verse 6? How are they still somewhat confused as to the nature of the Kingdom?

3. Read Mark 16:14-20, Matthew 28:16-20, Luke 24:44-53, and John 20:16-23. What direction was given to the disciples by Jesus? From these passages does it apply to the Church today? How?

4. From the following accounts what do you feel each author is trying to say? Mark 16:14-20; Matthew 28:16-20; Luke 24:44-53; John 20:16-23.

5. What do you find as the key verse in Acts 1:1-12 and why?

6. What did you find most helpful to you in this week's study?

Lesson 2: The Christian Community

1. From Acts 1:12-26, the first Christian community after Christ's ascension, comment on the significance of those present.

2. What do you find of importance in the election of Mathias?

3. From Acts 2:42-47, describe life in the early Christian community. What does that say to us today?

4. From Acts 4:23-35, what was it the community prayed for and how did God respond?

5. Do you think verses 32-37 belong with this arrest story or more appropriately with the first story of the next chapter?

6. What do you see as the function of the apostles in the chapter?

7. What do you think Acts 14:23 tells us about the early organization of the Christian community? (See also Acts 11:30.)

8. From these readings have you any added insights on your life as a Christian?

Lesson 3: Pentecost

1. Was there an outward appearance according to Scripture? What do you think it was? (Read Acts 2.)

2. Was the baptism of the Spirit for individuals or a body of believers?

3. What is meant by the gift of tongues? How does this affect us today? (Read Gen. 11:1-9; 1 Cor. 13-14.)

4. Are there any Old Testament parallels to the event of the first Pentecost?

5. What was the primary requirement for an apostle in the beginning? How does this apply to us today?

6. What was the substance of Peter's first sermon? Does it say anything to us today?

7. What did the study of this event in history mean to you this week?

Lesson 4: Conflict with Judaism

1. Read Acts 3 and 5. From Acts 3, what, if anything is the significance of Peter and John going into the temple for the prayer service?

2. Why does Peter begin his speech with, "The God of Abraham and of Isaac, and of Jacob, the God of our Fathers"?

3. From Acts 4:1-22, what was the charge that Peter and John were arrested on? Is this consistent with their interrogation the following day?

4. From Acts 5:17-24, what new element do you see entering into the arrest story in contrast to the one narrated in the previous chapter?

5. What was the reason behind the Sanhedrin's decision to release them? From Acts 4:1-22.

6. What is the function of the Spirit in 5:32? How do you think the Holy Spirit fulfilled this function then? How does He today?

Lesson 5: Stephen

1. Read Acts 6. What does Acts 6:1 tell us about the early Christian community which we haven't been told before?

2. What qualifications were considered necessary in those who were to be considered deacons

and how did these differ from the requirement considered necessary in the disciple who was to replace Judas among the twelve?

3. What similarities do you see between the arrest of Stephen and that of Jesus?

4. What do you think is Stephen's purpose in recalling the story of Joseph and Moses? (Read Acts 7.)

5. To what Old Testament figure do you think "The Righteous One" (7:59) refers?

6. Where do we hear a prayer similar to Stephen's dying prayer in 7:59? How does Stephen's prayer differ and what is the significance of this?

7. What do you see to be the religious significance of chapters 6 and 7 for us?

Lesson 6: Philip

1. Read Acts 8. Verse 1 refers to the persecution of the Church in Jerusalem. Was the Church present anywhere else at this time? (Notice how the places to which they were scattered are identical with those expressed in Acts 1:8.)

2. In preaching the word in a city of Samaria what was it that Philip proclaimed? Did that which Philip was doing in chapter 8 correspond to what he was commissioned to do in chapter 6 and verse 5?

3. What difference is there between the effects of baptism and the laying on of the hands in 8:14,17? Could this be an early expression of a rite we now call confirmation? (Cf. 6:6 for another rite of the laying on of hands.)

4. Why do you think Peter and John came down to Samaria?

5. How do you think Philip "starting with the scriptural text brought the eunuch to the Gospel of Jesus" (8:34)? Confer Isaiah 52:13—53:12 for the full context of the passage that the eunuch was reading.

6. Acts 8:37 is usually dropped from the text of Acts. Where do you think such a verse comes from and why was it added to the text?

7. What do you think is the point of this whole chapter for Luke? For us?

Lesson 7: Paul's Conversion

1. Read Acts 9. What similarities and differences do you observe in this account of Saul's conversion and in other New Testament accounts of the same event (Acts 22:3-16 and 26:4-18; Gal. 1:13-17)? How, if any way, do you think these differences and similarities help us to understand better the mystery of God's transformation of Saul?

2. What was it that Paul proclaimed in the synagogues?

3. What do you make of the differences between the Acts' account of Paul's first visit to Jerusalem and Paul's own account in Galatians 1:18-24?

4. What do you think is the significance of 9:31-43 which is sandwiched in between two decisive events in the early Church: Saul's conversion and Peter's baptism of the first Gentile (chapter 10)?

5. What did you find of religious significance or value in this chapter?

Lesson 8: Cornelius

1. Read Acts 10 and 11. In 10:4 who is Peter addressing as Lord? Who is the Lord in 10:14; in 10:33 and 10:36?

2. Compare the angel of God appearing in 10:4 with the angel of God appearing in Genesis 31:11-13. Who does the angel of God in the Genesis passage seem to be?

3. Compare Peter's attitude in 10:14 and 10:28 with his attitude expressed in the story Paul tells in Galatians 2:11-14. What do you think of all this? What is the religious significance for each of us?

4. What kind of an understanding of the mystery of the person and work of Jesus (i.e., Christological understanding) do you find expressed in 10:38? E.g., is this an affirmation of Jesus' divinity?

5. In 10:32-42 what did Peter say he and the other apostles were witnessing to? What did God command them to preach? To what did all the prophets bear witness?

6. Do you think most Christians appreciate what Peter says in 10:34? If what Peter says is true, then why be a Christian?

7. What did you find to be religiously important for you in this whole chapter?

Lesson 9: Peter

1. Read Acts 11 and 12. From Acts 11:1-3 what do you think Peter's authority in Jerusalem was at this time?

2. In Peter's defense of his actions (11:4-11), what do you think was the crucial point that silenced the doubts of those questioning him?

3. What was it that the refugees from Jerusalem proclaimed to the Greeks in Antioch? Is it similar to what Peter proclaimed to Cornelius' household in 10:34-43?

4. What do you make of what is said concerning the people's attitude in 12:2-3 and that which is expressed in 2:47, 4:21, 5:13, and 5:26?

5. Who does Peter say brought him out of prison?

6. Why do you think James is singled out in 12:17?

7. What do you find important in this lesson concerning your own spiritual growth?

Lesson 10: Council of Jerusalem

1. Read Acts 15. What is the point of controversy in 15:1—15:5? What is the solution given in 15:28-29?

2. Compare the controversy in 11:2-3 with Peter's defense there (11:5-17) and the effect of his defense (11:18) with this present controversy both in 15:1 and 15:5-6. Do you think the issue had really been satisfactorily settled before?

3. Notice the role of Barnabas in this struggle. See what Paul says about his conduct in Galatians 2:13. What do you make of this?

4. Who is Simeon in 14:14?

5. Whose recommendation wins approval and is put into the letter? What do you think this says about this individual (his importance) in the Jerusalem community?

6. 15:4 and 15:22 speak of the apostles, the elders, and the whole Church. What do you think this says about the whole Church? What do you think

this says about the present organization of the Jerusalem community?

7. Compare the necessary observances prescribed in the letter (15:29) with Paul's directions to the Corinthians in 1 Corinthians 8:1-13, 10:23-30 and to the Colossians in Colossians 2:20-23. What do you think this means?

8. Why do you think practices such as circumcision and dietary observances could be such a source of turmoil?

9. How did God reveal Himself to you through this chapter concerning a change in your personal life of Christian growth?

Lesson 11: The Missionary Journeys

1. Read Acts 13:1 — 14:28. What themes in these two chapters stand out as typically Lucan themes?

2. Why did Paul and Barnabas always go to the synagogues first (13:5,14 and 14:1)? Why did they feel justified in turning to the pagans?

3. Compare the structure and themes of Paul's speech (13:17-41) with those of Peter's speeches (e.g., 2:14-41). What does this say about the origin of the speeches in Acts?

4. Note the contrast of support and opposition that Paul and Barnabas experience. How is the term "the Jews" used? What do you think was behind the opposition of Jews, pagans, and authorities? Do we experience anything similar today?

5. Why did Paul and Barnabas react so strongly to the attitudes of the people in 14:11-13? One commentator has said about their words to the

crowd (14:14-18): "There is nothing specifically Christian in what they said." What do you think?

6. Read the accounts of Paul's second missionary journey (Acts 15:36—18:22) and third missionary journey (Acts 18:23—21:14). Note the similarities and differences in comparison with the first missionary journey (Acts 13:1—14:28). Do the second and third journeys add anything new *theologically* to the first?

7. What religious significance do the missionary journeys of Paul have for you?

Lesson 12: Imprisonment

1. What similarities do you see between what happened to Paul in Jerusalem and what happened to Jesus? What differences?

2. Paul has advised us to be all things to all men (1 Cor. 9:22—read 1 Cor. 8—10 on food offered to idols). How does Paul live this out himself?

3. What is the main line of defense that Paul takes before Felix, Festus, and Agrippa? How does Paul view the relationship between Judaism and Christianity? Has he changed his mind about freedom from the Law?

4. How would you square Paul's appeal to Caesar with the Gospel injunction: "Render unto Caesar the things that are Caesar's and unto God the things that are God's" (Mk. 12:13-17; Mt. 22:15-22; Lk. 20:20-26)?

5. What do you think is the most startling element in the account of Paul's journey to Rome? What do you make of it?

6. Why does Paul go to the Jews first in Rome

(28:17)? Why does he quote Isaiah 6:9-10 to them? What is the significance of the final verse in Acts (v. 31)?

7. In the whole Book of Acts, what did you find to be of greatest personal significance, i.e., what will you take home with you in the sense that it will become part of your life?

2

Paul's Letter to the Galatians

Lesson 1: Chapter One

This letter was written by Paul to his converts in Galatia during his third missionary journey, probably about 54-58 A.D. The key to this letter can be found in Acts 15: An account of the Council of Jerusalem (51 A.D.) at which it was decided that converts to Christianity did not have to observe the Mosaic law. A group of people, commonly called "Judaizers," evidently advocated circumcision and observance of the dietary laws as necessary to salvation. The "Judaizers" also cast doubt on Paul's teaching by saying that he was not really an apostle. Ancient Galatia was a Roman province in Anatolia, the plateau in the central part of Asia Minor. It lay off the mainstream of traffic and culture, and the people were peasants and mountaineers.

Chapter One: Paul defends the divine origin of his gospel by recounting the story of his conversion.

1. Read the opening chapters of Romans, and 1 and 2 Corinthians. How does the introduction to Galatians differ from these other letters? What does this difference tell us about Paul's attitude toward the Galatians?

2. How does Paul's account of his conversion as told by him in chapter 1:11-24 compare with Luke's account in Acts 9:1-19 and 22:3-6?

3. Why does Paul recount the story of his conversion and travels? Is he convincing?

4. From reading verse 10, what do you think the Judaizers were accusing Paul of doing?

5. What do you consider to be the most meaningful statement of Paul in chapter 1? Give reasons for your choice.

Lesson 2: Chapter Two

Paul continues to defend his gospel, and uses both personal incidents and early Church history to establish his point. He notes that his message was approved by Jerusalem (vs. 1-10), and he mentions Peter's inconsistency (vs. 15-21). It is not known whether the 14 years mentioned in verse 1 are computed from Paul's conversion, or from his first visit to Jerusalem.

1. In verse 4, when Paul refers to the "freedom we have in Christ Jesus" he means freedom from the Mosaic law of circumcision and from dietary restrictions. How would you define the "freedom we have in Christ Jesus" today, when we are not concerned with circumcision and dietary laws?

2. Contrast the characters of Peter and Paul as seen in chapter 2.

3. In verses 11-14, Paul rebukes Peter publically for giving the false impression that only Jewish Christians who observed the Levitical dietary laws were the real Christians. In your opinion, what effect do you think Paul's rebuke had on Peter's

attitude? On the "Judaizing" tendencies in the early Church?

4. In verse 16, what do you think Paul means when he says, "We are justified by the faith of Jesus Christ"? How would you define *justified?* What does the "faith of Jesus Christ" mean to you?

5. Explain your understanding of the statement: "Because of the law, I died to the law" (v. 19).

6. Summarize Paul's teaching on freedom from the law as found in verses 15-21.

7. Give a contemporary example of someone making the law more important than faith in Jesus Christ.

8. Verse 16: "We are justified by our faith and not by . . . doing the works of the law" seems to contradict the statement in James 2:14, "faith without right action is dead." Explain what you think Paul and James meant by these statements and determine whether their viewpoints differ.

Lesson 3: Chapter Three

In verses 1 to 28 Paul presents a scriptural defense of his doctrine. Two basic arguments are offered for faith replacing the law: one from the experience of the Galatians (vs. 1-5) the other from Scripture (vs. 6-26).

1. Discuss the relationship of Galatians 2:19 to 3:13 in the light of the quotation from Deuteronomy 21:23 (cited at the end of 3:13). What do you think these verses mean?

2. In 1:8 and 3:19 Paul refers to a common Jewish belief that the law was given to Moses by angels. Again in 3:7-18, Paul emphasizes Abraham

and the Jewish experience in arguments with a definite rabbinical character. Why would Paul include these passages in a letter to pagans who evidently (2:2) knew nothing of Jewish tradition or belief before their conversion?

3. In chapter 3, Paul gives at least four reasons (vs. 7, 15, 17, and 23) for faith to have replaced the law. Which of these reasons, in your opinion, would be the most compelling for the Galatians? For the Judaizers? Which one is the most convincing to you?

4. How would you reply to someone who said: " 'Putting on Christ' is just wishful thinking. What we need today are more people who keep the laws of the Church and of our country"?

5. In verse 28, Paul says that all the baptized are "one in Christ Jesus." What do you think Paul means when he makes this statement? What does it mean to you in today's world?

Lesson 4: Chapters 3:29—4:31

Paul continues his discourse on law and faith; he describes the reign of Christian freedom (3:29—4:20), and then cites an allegory from Scripture (4:21-31).

1. In verse 6, Paul says that without the Spirit a Christian would not be able to call God "Father." What does this mean to you personally?

2. What do we have to do to be God's sons/daughters and heirs?

3. Paul states that men were enslaved by both the law (3:24) and the elemental spirits (4:3) before Christ's coming. Even today we find much comfort

in the security of law and observing days and seasons. How would you answer Paul's question in verse 9?

4. In verses 13 and 14, Paul reminds the Galatians of his first preaching to them. What does this account tell you of Paul's relationship with the Galatians? Of their feelings for him?

5. Paul begins his argument from Scripture in verse 21 by saying: "If you want to observe the law, listen to it!" He goes on to equate Isaac, the child of promise, with the Gentile converts, who are also sons of Abraham "by faith." Then he asks in verse 30: "What does the Scripture say?" What implications do you think his answer in verse 31 has for the Judaizers?

Lesson 5: Chapters Five and Six

Paul's advice to the Galatians: He begins with a warning (5:1-12), gives instructions (5:13—6:10), and finally writes the conclusion (apparently in his own hand instead of that of his secretary) as a kind of signature.

1. Compare verses 5 and 6 (chapter 5) with James 2:18-19). How do these statements complement one another?

2. In 5:11, what kind of trouble does Paul refer to when he speaks of preaching the cross of Christ? Consult 1 Corinthians 1:23. What do you think this means in light of verse 11?

3. What effect could Paul hope to have on the Judaizers by comparing their insistence on circumcision with the ritual castration of the cult of Cybele alluded to in 5:12? (See also Phil. 3:2.)

4. Paul talks about "the whole Law" in 5:3 and 5:14. What do you think he means by these phrases in each instance?

5. What is the "spirit" mentioned in 5:16-18, and in 5:22-25? What effect does this spirit have on your everyday life?

6. Summarize your understanding of the law of love Paul sets down in chapter 6.

7. How is it possible for today's Christian to follow Paul's advice?

8. This letter has been called the "Magna Carta of Christian Liberty." Give reasons for agreeing or disagreeing with this title.

3

Mark

Introduction

This Gospel, attributed to Mark (identified with the John Mark of Acts 12:12 and 25) is the shortest of the Synoptic Gospels, and has often been called a passion narrative with a prologue. It was probably written after Peter's death (circa 64 A.D.) and before the destruction of Jerusalem (70 A.D.) *for non-Palestinian Christians of pagan origin.* It is divided into three main parts:

1. The Galilean ministry (1:14 to 6:5).
2. The journeys of Jesus (6:6 to 10:52).
3. The Jerusalem ministry (11:1 to 16:8).

Mark seems to have gathered together groups of narratives from oral tradition, and from personal testimony (probably Peter) to which he has added connections and summaries. The stories in Mark are noted for their vivid details.

Lesson 1 (1:1—1:20).

This section begins with John the Baptist, tells of Jesus' baptism, the temptation and beginning ministry, and ends with the calling of the first apostles.

1. What, in your opinion, is the significance of the "desert" in verses 3, 4, and 12? What is your personal desert?

2. Contrast John's baptism in verse 4 with that prophesized in verse 8. How did John's baptism differ from that of Christ as in Matthew 28:19?

3. Why do you think Christ submitted to John's baptism?

4. Discuss verses 10 and 11. What significance does this event have for Mark, considering its position at the beginning of his narrative? What does it mean to you personally?

5. What importance, if any, do you attach to the timing of Jesus' beginning of His preaching after the capture of John (v. 14)?

6. Why do you think that Simon, Andrew, James, and John followed Christ so quickly? What would be your reaction to such a call?

7. In your opinion, what is the "Good News," the Gospel, of verses 1 and 15? Has your own life been changed or affected by this good news?

Lesson 2 (1:21 — 1:45).

Jesus showed His authority in preaching and healing.

1. Define a miracle. What is a miracle to Mark? To you?

2. This section tells of three cures: 1. of a demonic; 2. of Simon's mother-in-law; 3. of a leper. Which of these three incidents has the most meaning for you? Why?

3. What is your personal reaction to demons and exorcism? (See vs 23, 32, and 34). Why do you feel as you do?

4. What seems to be the point of Christ's going into lonely places (1:35, 45b)?

5. Consider verses 31, 35, and 45a. What do these "actions" say to you about Christian life today?

6. Christ's preaching and teaching are mentioned in verses 15, 22, 27, and 38, yet little is really said about the message . . . what is being taught and/or preached? What reason can you give for this?

7. Discuss the verse in chapter one that has the most significance for you in your everyday life as a Christian.

Lesson 3 (2:1 — 3:6).

This section deals with Jesus demonstrating His authority in conflict with the Jews, and consists of five controversial episodes.

1. In verse 5 (chapter 2) *whose* faith was responsible for the cure of the paralytic? How can we apply the healing of the paralytic to our own lives?

2. Verse 10 (chapter 2) does not seem to fit into this conversation easily. The statement seems to be more properly addressed to the Scribes, yet Mark indicates Jesus was speaking to the paralytic. Why do you think Mark added this verse?

3. Compare the first two stories in this section in their concern with healing and forgiveness. (The paralytic and the calling of Levi.)

4. Contrast the call of Levi in 2:14 with that of the four apostles in 1:17 and 20. How are they similar? How do they differ? Which story impresses you the most? Why?

5. In 2:17, who are the "just"?

6. In your opinion, what is the significance of Jesus' answer to His detractors, the disciples of John who are fasting because of his death, concerning fasting as an ascetical practice (2:18-20)? Does fasting have any value for you personally?

7. In 2:21-22, Christ's sayings emphasize the "old" and "new." If we consider the "new" to be Jesus and His teachings, who are the "old"? John the Baptist? The Pharisees?

8. The cure of the man with the withered hand is the fifth story of Christ's conflict with the Jews in this lesson. What is there about this episode that would make it "the last straw" for the Pharisees (3:6)?

Lesson 4 (3:7—3:35).

This is the first part of a transitional section which spans the time between that of Jesus teaching the crowd to that during which He will concentrate on the instruction of his apostles.

1. What do verses 7-10 and 20 in chapter 3 tell us about the crowd and its relationship to Jesus? What effect did He have on the crowd?

2. Compare 3:7 to 1:5. In what way are they similar? How do they differ?

3. In 3:12 Jesus again asks for secrecy. Mark seems to emphasize the "Messianic Secret" (see also 1:25, 1:34, and 1:43), and yet in 2:10 and 2:28 Jesus calls attention to His power, and calls Himself "Son of Man." How can these statements in chapter 2 be reconciled to the "Messianic Secret"? Why do you think Mark's Gospel emphasizes this "Secret"?

4. In your opinion, what does verse 27 in chapter 3 say about Christ's power over Satan?

5. What does 3:29 mean to you? What does this sin seem to be?

6. 3:21 and 3:31-35 tell us about Jesus and His relatives. Compare His family's attitude toward Him with that of the crowds. Whose attitude is more justified, do you think? What do you think of Christ as He appears in Mark's Gospel by the end of the third chapter?

Lesson 5 (4:1—4:34).

This lesson consists of three parables, an explanation of a parable, and two sayings of Jesus as He teaches the crowds.

1. Concerning the parable of the Sower (4:2-8), what kind of "soil" has the word of God found in you?

2. What kind of "ears" (4:9) must one have to understand the Gospel today?

3. 4:12 is a quotation from Isaiah 6:9-10. What do you think this means in Mark? (See Mt. 13:14-15.)

4. It is commonly believed that 4:13-20, the explanation of the Sower parable, was added to the oral tradition in the early decades of the Church. Can you find any evidence of this from comparing the parable with the explanation? What motive could the early Church have had in adding this explanation?

5. 4:21-25 are actually four independent statements (given in different contexts in Matthew and Luke). If these statements (excluding v. 23) are considered separately, how would you explain each in terms of the coming of the Kingdom of God?

6. The Parable of the Seed (4:26-29) is found only

in Mark. Why do you think Mark included it here? What does this parable say to you personally?

7. Retell the Parable of the Mustard Seed so that its *meaning* is in a modern context.

Lesson 6 (4:35—6:6).

This lesson consists of four miracle stories that stress the need of faith.

1. Christ's calming of the sea (4:35-40) recalls the Old Testament stories of God conquering the sea (Gen. 1:2, Job 26:12, and Ps. 89:9) and saving His people (Ex. 15:19). How do you think the apostles, with some knowledge of the Old Testament stories, answered the question: "Who is this man" in verse 40? What answer, do you think, would have been given by a non-Christian hearing Mark's Gospel in the first century? What is your own answer after reading this story in Mark?

2. Keeping in mind that a boat was an ancient symbol for the Church, what do you think this story had to say to early Christians living in times of persecution?

3. The details of the story of the Gerasene demonic (5:1-20) seem to echo Isaiah 65:1-5. In your opinion, what is the significance of this story of the possessed man?

4. Christ does not ask for secrecy concerning the cure of the demonic (5:19) as with previous cures (1:35 and 1:43). Why?

5. Why do you think Mark inserts the story of the woman with a hemorrhage within the narrative of the cure of Jairus' daughter? The story (5:24-35) seems to dispel the idea that a kind of automatic

magic was responsible for Jesus' cures. What was responsible?

6. What do you think Jesus meant when He said: "The girl is asleep, not dead" in verse 39? What, in your opinion, is the significance of this miracle?

7. In chapter 5, Mark reiterates that faith is responsible for cures and miracles. What does the juxtaposition of these three miracle stories have to say about faith in Jesus by the people of Nazareth (6:1-6)?

Lesson 7 (6:7—6:44).

This section marks the beginning of the journeys of Jesus, wherein He devotes himself to teaching His apostles.

1. Compare 6:7 to 13:13-15. Explain.

2. What meaning do you find in Jesus' admonition to the apostles in 6:8-11? If the idea of poverty is *excluded*, what do you think Jesus is telling His apostles? What does this say to you in your life as a Christian today?

3. In the light of 6:35-44, what significance can you find in Jesus' charge (6:8) to take *no bread*?

4. The Herod vs. John the Baptist story (6:17-29) seems to have been inserted at this place in the narrative for a reason, since it logically would follow the event in 1:14. What purpose could Mark have in putting it here? Verses 16 and 19, marking the beginning and end of this story, seem to contain a message. How would you explain this message? What implications did John's death have for Jesus?

5. In 6:31, Jesus urges His apostles to withdraw

to the desert. What does this say to us in our life today? How much of ourselves can we afford to give in our ministry?

6. Find and explain the Old Testament symbols in the section on the feeding of the five thousand (6:34-44), and contrast them with the eucharistic symbols found here.

7. What do you think the story of the loaves and fishes means? What did it mean to Mark?

8. Are we open to the power of Christ in our lives, or are we "hard of heart" as Mark describes the apostles in 6:52? What is this hardness of heart? Is it the same for the Jews as the disciples? (See Mk. 3, 5, and 4:12.)

Lesson 8 (6:45—7:37).

A continuation of a catechesis (begun at 6:34) centered around the theme of bread.

1. Compare 6:45-52 with 4:35-40. In what ways are they different?

2. What is the point of the summary in 6:53-56? If you read this type of material in a biography, what would it say to you?

3. In 7:2, it is observed that Jesus' disciples no longer follow a strict interpretation of the law. What is the significance of the argument with the Pharisees in 7:1-8, especially in light of the feeding of the five thousand?

4. In your opinion, why was the pronouncement in 7:9-13 inserted within the story of obeying the Mosaic law? What meaning does it have for you?

5. The statements in 7:14-23 seem to answer the washing accusation in 7:1-9. What effect do you think this section would have on the early Church

when the controversy about observance of the Mosaic law was raging?

6. What meaning does the story of the Syro-Phoenician woman (7:24-30) have for you? Compare its main points with the story of the Gerasene demoniac, bringing out the similarities and differences.

7. What is the significance of "dogs" in 7:27-28 . . . of "bread" in these verses?

8. In the cure of the deaf-mute (7:31-37), in what way can the actions of Jesus effecting this cure be called "sacramental"?

9. How can you explain the excessive astonishment of the crowd over this cure, and its reference to Isaiah 35:5-6?

Lesson 9 (8:1—8:33).

This lesson consists of a section on the theme of bread that parallels the preceding lessons (6:35—7:37).

1. Contrast the feeding of the four thousand (8:1-10) with 6:34-44. List the similarities and differences.

2. Why does Mark include this story here, especially since it is so similar to, or perhaps identical with, the feeding of the five thousand? What does this miracle story say that wasn't said in 6:34-44?

3. Which of the two miraculous feedings says the most to you personally? Why?

4. 8:10-13 is a commentary on the Pharisees' reaction to Jesus' miracles. Would the Pharisees have recognized a sign if it had been given? Why didn't Jesus give them a sign?

5. Compare 7:1-23 with 8:10-13.

6. In the section 8:14-21, Jesus warns the apostles against being infected with the "yeast" of Herod, or wrong ideas about the role of the Messiah. If you had been an apostle at that time, what would you have answered when Jesus asked these questions which were designed to reveal the secret of God's kingdom?

7. Compare 8:22-26 with 7:31-37.

8. What is the significance of the gradual cure in 8:22-26? What relationship does the story of this cure have with the passage preceding it concerning the blindness of the apostles? What relationship does this story of the gradual cure have with Peter's declaration in the section following?

9. Peter's profession has been called the turning point of Mark's Gospel. Give reasons for agreeing or disagreeing with this statement.

Lesson 10 (8:27—9:29).

This lesson begins with Peter's profession of faith, continues with the first prediction of the passion and its sequels.

1. In 8:30, Jesus once again asks for secrecy. What significance can you find in this statement being closely followed by the first prediction of the passion (8:31) and the misunderstanding of the apostles (8:32-33)?

2. Peter shows by his actions in 8:33 that he really doesn't understand what being the Messiah means for Jesus. How do you understand the role of Jesus as Messiah? Describe your feelings about Jesus as the Suffering Servant (Is. 53).

3. What does the cross in 8:34 symbolize for you as a Christian?

4. Christ, in the six sayings in 8:34-38, sets forth arduous conditions for His followers. How do you view your own Christian commitments today in the light of Christ's conditions?

5. Compare the transfiguration of Jesus (9:2-9) with the Sinai experience of Moses (Ex. 24:15-18 and 34:29-30). What implications would this comparison have for the apostles?

6. What meaning can you find in the statement, "The cloud overshadowed them" (9:6) in the light of Old Testament symbols (cf. Ex. 16:10, 19:19, 24:15-16, and 32:9)?

7. Jesus' mention of His resurrection caused the apostles to wonder whether or not Elijah would come, as the Scribes predicted, before the resurrection of the dead. To whom do you think Christ referred when He said that Elijah had already come?

8. Jesus' exclamation in 9:18 doesn't really seem to fit this situation. What reason could Mark have for inserting it here?

9. In 9:24, the father of the epileptic boy makes a confession of faith. Compare this expression of belief with your own.

10. Compare the cure of the daughter of Jairus (5:38-42) with that of the epileptic boy. What is the significance of 9:26 and 27 in the boy's cure?

Lesson 11 (9:30—10:16).

The second prediction of the passion and its sequels.

1. How does the apostles' response to the second prediction of the passion (9:31) differ from the response to the first in 8:32b-33?

2. What do you think that Jesus is saying about Christian life to us now in 9:37?

3. Jesus' tolerance of the exorcist in 9:38-41 seems to belie the actions of the early Church regarding non-Christians' use of Jesus' name (as in Acts 8:18-24, 13:6-12, and 19:13-20). How can you explain this?

4. What significance could the sayings in 9:42-50 have had to Mark's audience—the first century Christians in Rome? What do they mean to you?

5. Compare Jesus' answer to the controversial questions of the Pharisees concerning divorce (10:1-12) with previous answers to such disputes in chapters 2 and 7. What do you find significant in the different kinds of answers?

6. Read 10:13-16. What is your own understanding of this section? How can we "welcome the Kingdom of God like a little child"?

Lesson 12 (10:17—10:52).

Continues the sequels to the second prediction of the passion and concludes with the third prediction and its sequels.

1. Jesus' words in 10:23 amazed and astonished the disciples because His idea was the complete reversal of the common Jewish idea that wealth was a sign of God's favor. What kind of emotions do Christ's words here stir in you?

2. How should Jesus' promise in 10:29-31 affect the manner in which we live our lives today?

3. Compare the three prophecies of the passion in 8:31-34, 9:30-32, and 10:33-34.

4. In 10:38, Jesus asks if James and John are

willing to suffer, as He will, by accepting the "cup" and "baptism." What would your answer have been?

5. Contrast 10:42-45 with 9:36-37. In your opinion, what is the most striking difference?

6. In 3:12 and 8:30, when Jesus is called by a messianic title, He asks for silence, yet in 10:47-48, He doesn't. Why not? What do you find different in the cure of Bartimaeus from that of the blind man in 8:22-26?

Lesson 13 (11:1 — 12:12).

This section marks the beginning of Jesus' ministry in Jerusalem.

1. Although in this section (11:1-10) Mark doesn't stress the fulfillment of a prophecy (Zech. 9:9) all of the circumstances of the entry into Jerusalem seem to point to this being a religious rather than a political event. What do you think that Jesus is saying by His mode of entrance into Jerusalem? How do you think the apostles looked on this triumphant entry? What was the attitude of the people of Jerusalem?

2. Discuss the significance of the story of the symbolic fig tree (11:12-14 and 11:20-25) as it relates to the fig tree as a figure of Israel. In chapter 5, Mark inserted the story of the woman with a hemorrhage within the narrative of the daughter of Jairus to emphasize the point of the second story. What reason could there be for inserting the story of the cleansing of the temple within the section about the symbolic fig tree?

3. When Peter asked why the fig tree withered,

Jesus answers: "Have faith in God" (11:22). What does this mean to you?

4. In 11:27-33, representatives of all groups of Jewish leaders question the authority of Jesus. The questioning takes the form of a rabbinical argument which ends in an impasse. What is the point of this story, in your opinion?

5. Discuss the implications of the parable in 12:1-9 as a summary for this whole lesson which illustrates Israel's rejection of Christ. (See Is. 5:1-7.)

6. Psalm 118 figures prominently in this lesson—it echoes the song sung by the people as Jesus entered Jerusalem (compare Ps. 118:26-27 with Mk. 11:10), and Jesus quotes Psalm 118:22 in Mark 12:10-12. What meaning does this have for you?

Lesson 14 (12:13—12:44).

The four last controversies of Jesus with the Jews: Herodians, Sadducees, and Scribes in which they attempt to discredit His teaching.

1. Compare 12:13 with 3:6. What are the implications for His detractors in Jesus' question in 12:15?

2. Christ's pronouncement in 12:17 (see Rom. 13:6-7) was given in answer to a question about a census tax. What was the point of this story for first century Romans—Mark's audience—who were not required to pay tribute?

3. The statement in 12:17 has been used to define the separation of Church and State—and,

sometimes, to excuse those who would argue against the Church's participation in civil affairs. What does this statement mean, in your own opinion?

4. The question posed by the Sadducees in 12:18-23, is designed to ridicule belief in resurrection, but Jesus points out that they don't even understand the little Scripture they accept as true, in their conservative orthodoxy. What meaning does Christ's answer in 12:26-27 have for you? What reaction did Christ's words evoke among the Sadducees, do you think?

5. Contrast the Scribe and his question in the section 12:28-34, with the Herodians and Sadducees and their questions in previous sections of this lesson.

6. What is the point of the question of Christ concerning the role of the messiah in 12:35-37a?

7. The section 12:37b-40 castigates the Scribes, yet in 12:28-34 Mark points out that a Scribe could easily believe in Jesus' teachings. What does this incident say to you in your own life today?

8. Contrast the character of the Scribe described in 12:37b-40 with that of the widow in 12:41-44. Jesus measures the worth of the widow's offering in terms of what she had to give. What implications does this have when we consider Christ's offering of Himself at the crucifixion?

Lesson 15 (13:1 — 13:37).

The eschatological discourse. 13:1-2 predicts the destruction of Jerusalem in 70 A.D.

1. 13:3-8 and 13:24-27 deal with the apocalyptic description of the final coming. Which of the events described seem to recur from time to time? How accurately can one predict the time of the parousia from this description?

2. The persecutions mentioned in 13:9-13 seem more realistically stated than the foregoing passage. What is your view of the persecutions mentioned here? Do you think this is part of being a Christian today, or is it only a description of the persecutions of the early centuries?

3. What does 13:11b mean to you? Has the Spirit ever spoken in your heart?

4. The abomination of desolation mentioned in the section 13:14-20 was a thing which destroyed because it defiled. The temple was defiled by the Syrian King Antiochus, and restored by the Maccabees. The prediction stated in this section came to pass at the destruction of Jerusalem after Mark's Gospel was written. What is the "abomination of desolation" today?

5. Compare 13:21-23 with 13:5-8. Are there false messiahs now?

6. Discuss 13:24-27. How are you preparing for the coming of the Son of Man?

7. In the section 13:28-37 there are several parables or sayings on vigilance: The fig tree, passing of the present generation and the world, unknown day and hour, and the servants and the householder. What is Mark telling us by these sayings on watchfulness about the way Christians must live?

8. What meaning do you find in the words in 13:22: "Not even the Son knows when the parousia will happen"?

Lesson 16 (14:1—14:21).

This section deals with the plot against Jesus, the anointing at Bethany, the preparation for the Passover, and the announcement of the betrayal.

1. The anointing at Bethany (14:3-9) seems to be another of Mark's sandwiched stories. Here, it is inserted in the story of the plot against Jesus (14:1-2 and 14:10-11). What reason, in your opinion, prompted Mark to juxtapose these stories?

2. The woman anointed the head of Jesus at the banquet in Bethany . . . a rather ordinary gesture in the Near East. What was incomprehensible, to the apostles, especially, was the great value of the ointment which cost ten months' wages. Jesus' answer implies that there is more to the idea of service than concern for the poor. What does the anointing at Bethany mean to you? What is the point of this story for Mark?

3. Discuss the implications of Jesus' statement in 14:9, when not even the name of the woman is given.

4. In 14:1-2, the enemies of Jesus decide that they will do nothing to Jesus during the feast days because they fear the reaction of the crowds. Why do you think they changed their minds in 14:11?

5. What motive do you think prompted Judas to seek out the priests in order to betray Christ? Discuss the character of Judas as seen in this lesson in Mark (up to 14:21).

6. Compare the events of the preparation for the Passover (14:12-16) with the preparation for Christ's entry into Jerusalem (11:1-6). In what ways are they alike? What do the stories say to you

about Christ? Do you think these events show a manifestation of divine foreknowledge, such as in, "You will meet a man carrying a pitcher of water . . ." in a place and time where men carried water in skins and women carried water in jugs; or, is this all just evidence of calm preparations made beforehand for the celebration of the feast? Which of these explanations and/or viewpoints has the most meaning for you?

7. In 14:18, Jesus' words recall Psalm 41:9— concerning the treachery of a table companion. What effect do you think Jesus' words in 14:21 had on Judas? What do you think Jesus meant by this statement?

Lesson 17 (14:22—14:42).

This section includes the institution of the Eucharist and the agony in the garden.

1. Compare 14:22 with 6:41 and 8:6. Which of the actions in 14:22 are common to all three selections? What do these actions mean to you?

2. Jews were forbidden to drink the blood of any creature, because blood represented life, and life belongs to God alone. In this context, what was the significance for the apostles of "drinking the blood" of Christ?

3. Mark 14:24 seems to echo Isaiah 53:11-12. In your opinion, what is the "new covenant" of which Jesus speaks? (See Ex. 24:8 and Jer. 31:31-34.)

4. 14:25 is an apocalyptic reference to the familiar theme of the messianic banquet. What do you think Christ meant by this statement—was He referring to His eating with His disciples after His

resurrection, or to some other time in the future? Does this "Kingdom of God" seem to be the same as in 1:15, 4:30, or 12:34? What does the "Kingdom of God" mean to you?

5. Discuss the section 14:29-31 as it reflects your own life.

6. Compare 14:34-37 with 13:33-37.

7. What does 14:36 say to you about the relationship between God the Father and Jesus?

8. What does this whole section 14:32-42 say to you about Christ? Consider particularly the implications of 14:33, 14:35, and 14:42. How does this picture of Christ differ from the Christ seen previously in Mark?

Lesson 18 (14:43—15:14).

This section begins with the arrest of Jesus, and includes the "trial" before the Sanhedrin, Peter's denials, and Jesus' appearance before Pilate.

1. Why do you think the chief priests, Scribes, and elders sent out their crowd at night to apprehend Jesus, especially since He had been in the temple at Jerusalem (14:49)?

2. Only Mark's Gospel tells us of the young man—who is not identified—but various sources have speculated that he was John the Apostle, James ("the brother of the Lord"), or John Mark, himself. Why do you think that Mark included this vignette?

3. According to Jewish law, at least two witnesses had to present testimony that agreed—and when this is not forthcoming—Jesus Himself is questioned by the Sanhedrin. At first, He is silent

(see Is. 53:7), but when asked if He is the messiah, He answers, "I am." What did this answer mean to Mark, especially in view of the messianic secret? What does it mean to you?

4. In what way was Jesus' statement in 14:62 considered blasphemy? (See Dan. 7:13 and Pss. 110:1 and 6.)

5. Compare the testimony of Peter in 14:68 and 14:71 with that of Acts 4:5-12. Do you consider Peter's denial cowardice, pride, or what? What do you feel is significant about Peter's denial?

6. Compare the "charges" of the Sanhedrin as they question Jesus in 14:61 and the accusation of Pilate in 15:2. Do you think that the Jews misunderstood Jesus' message concerning the role of the messiah enough to think that He was attempting to be crowned the King of the Jews, or did they simply wish to get rid of Him and use His claim to being the Messiah as a political charge against Him to the Romans?

7. Do you think that Pilate and the Jewish leadership were in collusion to condemn Jesus to execution? Give reasons for your answer.

8. Pilate thought that the Jews had delivered Christ to him out of envy (15:10). What do you think their motives were?

9. Contrast Pilate's treatment of Jesus in 15:2-5 with that of the crowd in 15:13-14.

Lesson 19 (15:15—15:41).

This section begins with the scourging and includes the crucifixion and death of Jesus.

1. Compare 14:65 with 15:16-19. Discuss your feelings after reading these sections.

2. It's probable that Jesus was unable to carry the crossbeam of the cross (the upright was permanently fixed at the execution site), especially after the scourging; but it was uncommon to have someone else carry it, other than the condemned one (15:21). What does this verse say to you, especially in light of 8:34?

3. Read Psalm 22. Compare Psalm 22:1-18 to Mark 15:24-32. In 15:34, Jesus cries out the opening lines of Psalm 22. Do you think that this is a cry of despair or a prayer of hope?

4. 15:39 marks the climax of Mark's Gospel. What do you think the centurion meant by these words? In your opinion, what was Mark's meaning? After reading and meditating on 15:15-41, what do the words in 15:39 mean to you personally?

5. What significance do you find in Mark's statements concerning the women (15:40-41)?

6. Which of the events recorded in this lesson impresses you the most? Why?

Lesson 20 (15:42—16:20).

This lesson includes the burial of Jesus, and the discovery of the empty tomb, as well as the canonical ending of the Gospel.

1. What evidence can you cite from Mark's Gospel that Jesus really died?

2. What, in your opinion, were the motives of Joseph of Arimathea in asking for the body of Jesus?

3. The resurrection itself is not recorded, just the discovery of the empty tomb. What does the empty tomb symbolize for you?

4. What meaning can you find in the recording of the names of the women in 15:40, 15:47, and 16:1? Do you think that 16:1 has any relation to 14:8? Why?

5. Compare Christ's prophecy in 14:27-28 with the events of the days following and the angel's words in 16:7. What significance does Galilee have for Mark in these verses?

6. Compare the literary style of the canonical, but non-Markan, ending (16:9-20) with the rest of Mark's Gospel. In what ways do you think they differ?

7. Read Acts 1:1-11. Compare the events recorded there with Mark 16:9-20.

8. In your opinion, what has impressed you the most in reading and studying Mark's Gospel? How has Mark's Gospel changed you?

4

John

Lesson 1 (1:1—1:51).

1. What does verse one say to you personally about the *Word's* existence before the incarnation, His relationship to the Father, and His Divinity?

2. How was the baptism of John different from the baptism instituted by Jesus (Jn. 1:26-33 and Mk. 1:4)?

3. A. Why did the Pharisees ask John if he was Elijah (Mal. 4:5-6 and 2 Kings 2:11)?

   B. Why did John not see himself in this role although Jesus later ascribed it to him (Mt. 11:14 and Mk. 9:9-13)?

   C. What does John teach us through his disclaimer?

4. What do you imagine could have transpired that evening (Jn. 1:39-41) that resulted in so radical a change in Andrew, leading him to exclaim to his brother Simon: "We have found the Messiah!"? Think about this in terms of Matthew 11:2-6 and Isaiah 29:18-19, which describe the Messiah's mission in life. Have you ever had an encounter with God that changed your life "overnight"?

5. In the calling of the disciples, why was it seemingly simple for them to follow Jesus so readily and without question and for others to reject Him so vehemently?

6. What do you think of Nathanael's remark: "Nazareth! Can anything good come from there" (Jn. 1:46)? Do you have a "Nazareth" in your life?

Lesson 2 (2:1—3:21).

1. The events of the life of Jesus are the mystery of God revealing Himself to us. As you listen to the story of the wedding at Cana (Jn. 2:1-11), what do you hear God telling you about Himself?

2. The last word of Mary, Jesus' mother, recorded in the Gospels are: "Do whatever He (Jesus) tells you" (Jn. 2:5). What do you hear the Spirit saying to you in this verse?

3. What meaning does the cleansing of the temple have for us today (Jn. 2:13-17)?

4. Why do you suppose it was only after Jesus had been raised from the dead that His disciples recalled His words of John 2:19 and came to believe? Have you ever had the experience of understanding an event in your life only at a later date (Jn. 2:18-22)?

5. In John 3:1-2 what meaning can you see in Nicodemus' coming to Jesus at night? (Also read Jn. 13:30 and Ps. 139:11-12.)

6. In John 3:8 what does "the wind chooses where to blow" mean to you?

7. John 3:3-10 deals with Nicodemus, a scholar and teacher, questioning Jesus' teaching on the necessity of spiritual rebirth. In view of Mark 8:18

and Mark 10:23-27, does anything in your life keep you from hearing and understanding God's words?

8. The Nicodemus discourse concludes in John 3:21: "He who acts in truth comes into the light." What is the "truth" here? What is the "light"?

9. Which of the events recorded in this lesson had the most meaning for you personally? Why?

Lesson 3 (3:22—4:54).

1. A. Why were John's disciples upset that people were flocking to Jesus (Jn. 3:26)?
   B. How do you feel when people to whom you minister seek the Lord from others?

2. "He (God) does not ration His gift of the Spirit" (Jn. 3:34). If this is true, how do you account for the appalling absence of God's Spirit in so many areas of modern life, and in areas of your own life?

3. It is a common human fear that loving means taking the risk of being depleted, emptied. In John 3:35, we are told that "The Father loves the Son and has given *everything* over to Him." The obvious implication is that the Father can give everything in love without losing anything of Himself. From your own experience, what have you learned about this mystery? Can you give yourself to one you love without losing your own fullness as a person?

4. After Jesus told the Samaritan woman what He knew of her past, we see in John 4:19 that she changed the subject. Why do you think she did this?

5. In John 4:36 what is meant by "he who sows and he who reaps shall rejoice together"? Compare this with 1 Corinthians 3:6-9.

6. In John 4:44 Jesus declares that there is no respect for a prophet in his own country. What does He mean? (See Mt. 23:37; Jn. 5:45-47; Acts 7:52, and Mk. 6:4.)

7. Read for the context John 3:25-30. In 3:27 we read: "No one can lay hold on anything unless it is given from on high." How is this realized or not realized in the chapters thus far covered:

    A. In John the Baptist?
    B. In the first disciples?
    C. In Mary at Cana?
    D. In Nicodemus?
    E. In Jesus?
    F. In John the Evangelist?
    G. In the woman at the well?
    H. In the royal official?
    Pick as many as you wish.

Lesson 4 (5:1 — 6:15).

1. In 5:6 Jesus says to the sick man: "Do you want to be healed?" What did the man have to do to be healed? When Jesus asks me the same question: "Do you want to be healed?" what must I do to be healed?

2. In John 5:14, what did Jesus' warning mean to you regarding conversion?

3. In John 5:16, Jesus' answer to the Jews over the Sabbath controversy was: "My Father goes on working and so do I." What do you think Jesus meant by this?

4. John 5:44 deals with man being satisfied with human glory instead of eternal glory. Discuss several examples of human glory our society strives for. Are there perhaps some in your own life?

5. Just as Jesus multiplied the five barley loaves and two fishes, He can multiply our works. The little we do for the Lord's sake can affect many. How do you experience the fragments of your life being gathered up so that nothing is lost?

6. In 5:24 Jesus says: "I solemnly assure you, the man who hears my word and has faith in Him who sent me possesses eternal life. He does not come under condemnation, no, he has passed from death to life." (Compare Rom. 8:1-3, 1 Jn. 3:14, Jn. 4:39-42, and Jn. 4:50.) In the context, what does this tell about Jesus? About Sabbath law? About Jesus' audience at that time? What about me?

Lesson 5 (6:16—6:71).

1. One of the most powerful recurring themes in both the Old and New Testaments (Is. 43:5) is expressed in verse 6:20: "It is I; do not be afraid."
   A. Why do you think God felt it necessary to repeat Himself so often on this matter of fear?
   B. What do you hear Him saying to you about the world situation, about the Church, about your own personal life?

2. In John 6:26 Jesus' answer reveals much about the crowd. How did the crowd's expectations differ from yours?

3. In verse 6:27 Jesus declares that the Father, God Himself, has set His seal on Him. What other scriptural testimony do we have of this fact?

4. John 6:51 states: "I myself am the living bread that came down from heaven. If anyone eats this bread, he will live forever." In the physical world eating is a necessary act responding to a felt need. How do we come to know the need of our hearts?

93

5. In John 6:63 Jesus said: "It is the spirit that gives life; the flesh is useless. The words that I have spoken to you are both spirit and life."

    A. What is being taught here (Neh. 9:20; Jn. 3:8, 14:26; and Rom. 8:16)?

    B. What does this say to you?

6. The eucharistic discourse throughout this section seems to affect people differently. What do you think the effect of this discourse is on the following:

    A. The people of 6:24?

    B. The Jews in 6:41?

    C. His followers in 6:60?

    D. Peter in 6:68?

    E. Judas in 6:71?

    F. Me in 6:24-71?

7. What does John say in this lesson about salvation? How do you personally feel salvation can be achieved?

Lesson 6 (7:1—8:59).

1. What do you think Jesus meant (Jn. 7:6-7) when He said: "The right time for me has not yet come, but any time is right for you"?

2. In 7:24 what do you think was the real meaning behind Jesus' words: "Do not keep judging according to appearances; let your judgment be according to what is right"? As you reflect over your life, how do you feel these same words could apply to you?

3. John 7:40-43 deals with the confusion of the multitudes as to Jesus' identity. Due to the various preconceived ideas about His origin, can you think

of prejudices or biases that would keep you from recognizing Jesus were He to appear before us now? Do you recognize Him dwelling in each person you meet? How?

4. If we Christians are not to condemn one another unless we are *without sin*, what should our attitude be toward our fellow Christians and toward non-believers (1 Cor. 5)?

5. In John 8:12-20 there is one sentence that pinpoints why God became man in Jesus. What do you think it is and why?

6. In John 8:12 Jesus states: "No follower of mine shall *ever* walk in darkness; no, he shall possess the light of *life*." How then do you account for the times when you seem to be "in the dark"; for example, about God's will for you or about why He is allowing a rash of trials to hit you all at one time (Jn. 10:10)?

7. Why does Jesus not condemn the adulterous woman at the beginning of chapter 8 and yet is critical of the Jews in the temple (Jn. 8:31-59)?

8. What did you find most meaningful and helpful to you personally in this lesson and why?

Lesson 7 (9:1—10:42).

1. In John 9:39-41 Jesus explains to the Pharisees His mission regarding their blindness. How does the Spirit today try to bring light to the modern Pharisee, the one who will not see?

2. In John 10:2-3 Christ the Good Shepherd enters the sheepfold (the world) and calls to His sheep. With this in mind:

A. How did Christ's voice reach you?

B. Discuss the ways in which Christ's voice reaches His people.

C. Who are Christ's sheep?

3. In John 10:10 Jesus says: "I have come that they might have life and that they might have it more abundantly." What does this abundant life mean to you?

4. In John 10:27-28 Jesus says: "The sheep that belong to me listen to my voice. I know them, and they follow me. I give them eternal life. They will never be lost and no one will ever steal them from me." What does He mean; about whom is He talking?

5. List the qualities of one in authority as symbolized by the shepherd in 10:1-18. Contrast those qualities with those of the Pharisees in chapters 9 and 10. What other leadership qualities do you look for in your church?

6. Trace the growth of faith on the part of the man born blind (Jn. 9:1-41). Share any experience you may have had in which deeper faith grew out of suffering or severe trials.

Lesson 8 (11:1—12:50).

1. Why did Jesus' restoration of Lazarus' life lead to His own death?

2. Throughout history some Christians have quoted John 12:8 as proof that it is God's will that society be divided into "haves" and "have nots."

A. What does the Church teach about this?

B. What do you personally believe?

3. Let's look at Mary's anointing of Jesus (12:1-8) on two levels:

A. What do you think it meant symbolically to Jesus as the Messiah (Mk. 14:3-9)?
B. What do you think it meant to Jesus the man?

4. Why did the chief priests plan to kill Lazarus also? Is there more significance to this than meets the eye?

Challenge Question:

5. In John 12:20-36 Jesus foretells His death and glorification. How could He do this? Several other historical figures have alluded to their coming deaths, including Joan of Arc and Martin Luther King. Do you see any similarities?

6. How does the passage (12:37-43) encapsulate Jesus' ministry:
A. To the Jewish leaders?
B. To Nicodemus (3:1-15)?
C. To Caiaphas (11:49-53)?

7. To what commandment is Christ referring in John 12:49-50 (see also 1 John 3:23)? Do you know a religious song that expresses one of the themes of this commandment?

8. As Jesus appears in chapters 11 and 12 of John's Gospel, He is the resurrection: the source, the substance, and the first fruits. Christ comes to us and calls us to Himself. How would you explain this in terms of your life here and in the hereafter?

Lesson 9 (13:1—14:31).

1. John was the only writer who reported the account of the foot washing at the Last Supper (Jn. 13:4-11).

A. What message do you think John was trying to pass on to us?

B. What are some of the ways in which we could wash each other's feet?

2. "Judas accepted the bread and went out at once. It was night" (John 13:30). What does this passage mean to you?

3. Why did Jesus call the apostles "My little children" in John 13:33? What Christian implications does this have for you, if any?

4. In John 14:12-14 Jesus promises that those who believe in Him will do *greater works* even than He has done. Have you experienced or are you familiar with works such as these being performed today?

5. Explain how the Lord manifested Himself to the apostles (Jn. 14:17-24). How does He manifest Himself to you?

6. If the Father and the Son are equal (Jn. 1:1-2), why does Jesus say that "The Father is greater than I" (Jn. 14:28)? (See Phil. 2:5-8.)

7. Chapter 14 gives us the great teaching on the mystery of the divine indwelling of the Holy Spirit. Read also Colossians 1:24-29. How do you personally experience this Living Presence in your life?

Lesson 10 (15:1—17:26).

1. In John 15:18-16:4 Jesus warns of the persecution His disciples will suffer at the hands of the Jews.

A. Why do you think the Jewish leaders hated Jesus so?

B. Why did they persecute His disciples?

C. What good do you see coming from the hostility of the "world" to early Christianity?

2. How does John show the working of the Trinity in 16:4b-15?

3. John 16:23 begins with: "And in that day you will ask me no question." To what day is Christ referring? (See Jer. 31:31-34.)

4. Christ prays for those who are His (Jn. 17:6): "You gave them to me"—as sheep to the shepherd, to be kept; as a patient to the physician, to be cured; as children to a tutor, to be taught. How does Jesus reach you?

5. What do you think is a Christian's relationship to the world in terms of John 17:14-18, John 15:19, and Matthew 28:19-20?

6. What qualities are emphasized by John 17:20-26 as truly important to Jesus in His prayers to the Father?

7. Chapter 15 is a discourse on union with Christ and chapter 16 is a discourse on the coming of the Advocate.
   A. What do you feel is the key phrase in each chapter?
   B. What does each of these phrases say to you personally in your life today?

Lesson 11 (18:1—19:5).

1. In the scene of Jesus' betrayal by Judas (Jn. 18:1-12), with which of the characters do you identify and why?

2. In John 18:19-20, Jesus said: "I have spoken openly to the world. In secret I have said nothing." How can you justify this with: "To you (the disci-

ples) it is given to know the mysteries of the kingdom of heaven, but to them it is not given" (Mt. 13:10-15 and Mk. 4:10-12)?

Challenge Question:

3. Reflect prayerfully on the passages of Peter's denial of Jesus (Jn. 18:17-18 and Jn. 18:25-27; also see Mt. 26:69-75; Mk. 14:66-72; and Lk. 22:54-62). What is Peter denying and affirming? Share what the Spirit gives you to understand about this.

4. How does Pilate represent the tragedy of trying to be neutral when confronted with Jesus (Jn. 18:33-40)? Contrast him with the Samaritan woman of John 4:1-26.

5. Jesus was killed not because He claimed to be king, but because He bore witness to "the truth" (Jn. 18:26-38). What is this truth?

6. In John 19:1-5 Jesus is made to appear like a complete fool by Pilate and his soldiers. In 1 Corinthians Paul reminds Christ's followers that, in view of the pagan society around them, they appear as foolish as Jesus did and must expect no better treatment (1 Cor. 3:18-19 and 4:9-10). How do you understand your life as a Christian in these terms? In what ways do you appear to be foolish in the eyes of your neighbors as you try to live by what you believe?

7. During the course of His passion, Jesus was deprived of His freedom by being arrested and handcuffed. Then He was successively stripped of His civil rights and His dignity as a human being. Finally, life itself was taken away in a must cruel

manner. What do you feel about this injustice? What do you feel, and what should we do about injustice in our prison system today? (See Mt. 25:34-46.)

Lesson 12 (19:6—19:42).

1. Why was Jesus (Paul, Dietrich Bonhoeffer and others) fearless in the face of torture and death? (See Jn. 10:17-19 and 19:10-11 and Mt. 10:28.)

2. Most of us hear the story of Christ's crucifixion every year at Easter. After having made this study of John's Gospel, how has your understanding of this event been changed? Please share any new insights you have.

3. None of the Gospels record that the apostles were with Jesus on Calvary except the beloved disciple; instead, there were the women who accompanied Him. Why? Where do you think His apostles were at this supreme moment?

4. In John 19:34-35 we learned that when Jesus' side was pierced, blood and water poured out. What significance do you find in this?

5. In John 19:1-16 Pilate, in the role of judge, attempts in vain to harmonize equity and injustice in dealing with Christ's deliverance into the hands of the Jews. How do you act like Pilate, measuring equity and injustice rather than love?

6. Each of the four Gospel writers treats of our Lord's death with more or less fullness of detail, whereas His birth and several of His miracles and discourses are found in only one or two of the Gospels. Why do you think this is so?

7. Meditatively ponder John 20 and share your reactions and personal witness of Jesus' resurrection in: Peter, John, Mary Magdalene, Thomas, the rest of the disciples. (See Luke 24:13-35.)

Lesson 13 (20:1—20:31).

1. "The Lord has been taken from the tomb" cried Mary, "we don't know where they have put him!" (Jn. 20:2). When you want to find the risen Lord, where do you look?

2. In John 20:14-15 Mary Magdalene does not recognize Jesus until in verse 16 He calls out her name. How would you explain this? (See Jn. 10:3-5; 1 Cor. 15:42; and Lk. 24:31-35.)

3. Some scholars wonder why, on this great resurrection day, Jesus gave the disciples the power to forgive sin. Share your thoughts on this from what you have learned from John's Gospel message (Jn. 20:23).

4. In John 20:21-23, what relationship do you see between this incident and the whole concept of community reconciliation?

5. The resurrection appearances and the entire Gospel narrative itself are testimony of the first Christians to what they had seen. In light of this, what is "belief" and what do you think Jesus meant when He said: "You believe because you can see. Happy are those who have not seen and yet believe"?

6. In John 20:31 John said, ". . . that believing you may have life in His name." If John means "life" as discipleship to Jesus, participant in the King-

dom of God, what event or events in your life made you aware that you were called to a life in Christ?

Lesson 14 (21:1—21:25).

1. How does the incident of the miraculous catch of fish (Jn. 21:1-14) demonstrate the difference between doing God's work when and how we want and depending upon God for direction and guidance?

2. Jesus said to Peter in John 21:15-17: "Do you love me more than these?" What evidence do you find in Scripture of the love that prompts Peter to reply: "You know that I love you"? If Jesus would ask you the same question, what evidence could you produce?

3. It is the will of Christ that His disciples should not be curious about future events. In John 21:22 He tells them: "You are to follow me." What meaning do these words have for you personally? (See Mk. 13:32-37 and Jn. 1:38-43.)

4. In John 21:7-8 when Peter was aware that it was the Lord on shore, he jumped into the water and went to the Lord. After studying all of John's Gospel, would you consider yourself like Peter—impulsive, quick to assert yourself? Do you run to Christ or do you wait to be greeted? Share your feelings on this with your group.

5. The primacy of Peter in the apostolic community is a common teaching of the Gospels. In this last chapter of John's Gospel, Christ is even more explicit in designating Peter as shepherd of His flock. What type of life was Peter commissioned to? What does this say to you personally?

6. At the conclusion of the Gospel (Jn. 21:25) the author explains that not everything has been written about what Jesus did. Are you longing to know more about Jesus or are you satisfied with what knowledge you have?

5

Matthew

Lesson 1 (1:1—1:25).

This section includes the geneology of Christ and the annunciation to Joseph.

1. The geneology of Joseph cited in Matthew 1:1-17 presents three groups of fourteen generations of ancestors from David to Joseph. Its purpose is to show that Jesus was a son of David. Why do you think this fact would be important to the people for whom Matthew wrote his Gospel?

2. Besides Mary, the mother of Jesus, four women are mentioned in this geneology: Tamar (v. 3) who was a Canaanite, Rahab (v. 5) a Canaanite, Ruth (v. 5) a Moabite, and Bath-Sheba (v. 6, "former wife of Urias") who was a Hittite. Why do you think that Matthew included these women, all non-Jews, in this geneology?

3. Discuss how you think Joseph felt when he found out Mary was pregnant. Include the following in your discussion: (A) How do you think Joseph found out about Mary's pregnancy? Do you think Mary told him, or someone else? (B) Do you think he felt that since Mary was pregnant by the Spirit, he should humbly withdraw, or he should put Mary

away because he didn't believe she was pregnant by the Spirit?

4. The question of how Joseph's geneology could show that Christ is a son of David is answered in 1:20-21. Joseph is to adopt Mary's son and provide for him a royal lineage. Discuss the significance of the name Joseph is to give Mary's son: Jesus (or Joshua, "Yahweh saves"). Do you think that Joseph and Mary realized the significance of Jesus' name?

5. In 1:23 Matthew cites Isaiah 7:14 as proof that Christ's birth was foretold by the prophets. What is your understanding of the name Emmanuel ("God with us") as applied to Christ? What do you think it meant to Mary and Joseph?

Lesson 2 (2:1—2:23).

This section completes the prologue to Matthew's Gospel, and includes the story of the Magi, the flight into Egypt, and the slaughter of the innocents.

1. The story of the Magi is filled with Old Testament symbols. Compare Matthew 2:2 with Numbers 24:17, and Matthew 2:11 with Isaiah 60:6 and Psalm 72:10. In 2:6, Matthew quotes Micah 5:2. What meaning do these Old Testament symbols have for you? What meaning do you think they had for the early Church?

2. Discuss the impact tradition has had on the details of the Magi story as found in Matthew (that is, the tradition that they were "three kings").

3. Compare 2:3 with 2:11. What point do you think Matthew is making with this story?

4. Compare Exodus 1:2 with Matthew 2:16 and Exodus 4:19 with Matthew 2:20. What meaning do you think these allusions had for Matthew's first century readers?

5. Discuss what you find significant about messages in dreams in the first two chapters of Matthew. (See 1:20, 2:12, 2:13, 2:19, and 2:22.)

Lesson 3 (3:1—3:17).

The third chapter of Matthew is the beginning of Book One: The Proclamation of the Reign. This lesson is the first part of the narrative section on the beginning of the ministry, and includes the preaching of John the Baptist, and the baptism of Jesus.

1. Compare Matthew 3:1-12 with Mark 1:1-8. How do they differ?

2. What does John's message in 3:2 mean to you? What do the words "repent" and "kingdom of heaven" mean to you?

3. Read 2 Kings 1:8. What point do you think Matthew is making in 3:4?

4. What meaning can you find in the eschatological symbols mentioned by John the Baptist in 3:7-12: "fruit," "fire," "winnowing fan," "wheat," and "chaff"?

5. Jesus comes to John for baptism. Since John is calling sinners, why does Jesus respond? Is his life changed? How has your life been changed in response to this call? What does baptism mean today?

6. What is Matthew trying to say in 3:16-17? How does this account differ from Mark 1:9-10?

7. In 3:14-15, what insight do you think Jesus and John had concerning their respective roles in salvation?

Lesson 4 (4:1—4:25).

This lesson is the completion of the narrative section of Book One, and includes the temptation of Jesus, the first proclamation in Galilee, the call of the first disciples, and the journey in Galilee.

1. Explain your understanding of the Old Testament symbols in 4:1-11: the desert, forty days, hunger, the mountain. (See Num. 11:5-9.)

2. Why do you think Matthew elaborates on the temptation story? (See Mk. 1:12-13.) What do you think the temptations symbolize? What is Matthew saying about temptation to power to the early Church? . . . to the Church today?

3. What does Jesus' proclamation in 3:17 mean to you?

4. What significance do you find in the fact that Jesus began His preaching in Galilee? What did Matthew find important about Galilee? (See 3:15.)

5. Compare Matthew 4:18-22 with Mark 1:16-20. What does the phrase "fishers of men" mean to you? (See Jer. 16:16.) What point do you think Matthew is making with this story?

6. How do you think the response of the apostles to Jesus' call compares to the reaction of today's people to a vocation or call?

7. Discuss the comparison of Matthew 4:23-25 with Mark 1:14, 21, 28, 32-34, 39, and 3:7f-8.

Lesson 5 (5:1—5:20).

This lesson is the first part of the discourse section of Book One: The Sermon on the Mount.

1. What Old Testament figure is brought to mind by the use of the mountain in 5:1?

2. Compare the first four Beatitudes (5:3-6) with the next four (5:7-10). How does the first group differ from the second? Which types of people are talked about in each group?

3. Paraphrase the Beatitudes in modern times. What does "poor in spirit" mean?

4. Compare 5:3-13 with Isaiah 61. What effect do you think Christ's preaching on the Beatitudes had on a people familiar with Isaiah 61 as a prophecy of the messianic times?

5. In verses 13-16, Christ describes the apostolic vocation as a calling that "salts" and "lights" the earth. What do these figures of speech mean to you when used to refer to the apostles in Jesus' time? What is the function of an apostle today?

6. Explain 5:16 in your own words.

7. What is your interpretation of the word "fulfill" in 5:17?

8. How can you reconcile Jesus' teaching in Matthew 5:19 with His actions in Mark 7:1-5? How do you work out this dilemma personally?

Lesson 6 (5:21—6:18).

A continuation of the Sermon on the Mount. The first part of the lesson deals with the law and the Gospel of Christ. The law is seen as an impersonal set of rules for the conduct of a people, while the Gospel puts this rule of conduct on a personal level. The second part of the lesson contrasts genuine Christian righteousness with the spurious righteousness of the Pharisees.

1. Discuss 5:23-24. What is Jesus saying here about the primacy of reconciliation? In these verses, who is urged to initiate reconciliation, the one sinned against, or the sinner? Why?

2. What do you think Jesus means with His statement in 5:29-30?

3. What does 5:39-42 say to you in your everyday life as a Christian? In what ways can we implement these examples in our activities?

4. Contrast 6:1-4 with 5:16. In what ways do they differ?

5. Discuss the relationship between private and public prayer and ways of resolving the tension between them (6:5-8).

6. Paraphrase the Lord's Prayer in modern terms. What purpose do you think this prayer serves, coming at this point in Matthew's Gospel?

7. In 6:16-18, do you think that Jesus is in favor of fasting or against it?

Lesson 7 (6:19—7:29).

This lesson concludes the discourse section of Book One (Sermon on The Mount) with a collection of detached sayings.

1. Verses 19-21 speak of "treasure." What kind of "treasure" can we store up in heaven?

2. Restate 6:22-23 in terms of "the Christian is a light to the community."

3. The sayings in 6:19-24 seem to concentrate on one Christian attitude. What do you think this attitude is, and how does it fit into the context of the rest of the chapter?

4. How does the passage on solicitude (6:25-34) speak to you in the experience of your own life?

5. Discuss the difficulties in your own life with the temptation to judge others by giving an example of the plank in your own eye.

6. How can we reconcile 7:6 with Jesus' commission to go out and spread the Good News to the whole world?

7. How do you pray? Do your experiences fit the description of Matthew in 7:7-11, or has God put you on hold?

8. 7:20 seems to contradict 7:1. Discuss.

9. 7:24-27 seems to say that if a person hears and understands what is said, he must act on it. Explain why you agree or disagree with this interpretation.

Lesson 8 (8:1 — 8:27).

This section is the beginning of Book Two: The Ministry in Galilee. Lesson 8. is the first part of the narrative section: the cycle of ten miracles.

1. Compare the cure of the leper in Matthew 8:1-4 with that in Mark 1:40-45. In what ways do they differ? In discussing the differences, try to find a reason for Matthew's use of this story.

2. What do you think is the essential condition for the miracles in 8:1-13?

3. Compare Matthew 8:14-15 with Mark 1:29-31. What reason do you think the author of

Matthew could have for calling the apostle *Peter*, rather than Simon, as Mark did?

4. What reason do you think Matthew is giving for Jesus' cures in 8:16-17?

5. What conditions does Jesus lay down for being a disciple in 8:20 and 22? How can you reconcile His demand in your everyday life as a Christian disciple?

6. What may we expect the Lord to do for us when we get into "rough seas" (8:23-27)?

Lesson 9 (8:28—9:34).

This lesson continues the miracle stories that make up the narrative section of Book Two.

1. Compare Matthew 8:28-34 with Mark 5:1-17. Discuss. Explain your understanding of 8:29. What reason can you find for the inclusion of this statement in Matthew's Gospel?

2. Discuss the relationship between sin and disease in the early Church. What does faith in Jesus accomplish for the paralytic in 9:1-8? What does faith in Jesus do for you personally?

3. Find a current example of the story of the Pharisees condemning Jesus for associating with sinners.

4. Read Hosea, chapter 6. What do you think Jesus meant when He said: "I want mercy, not sacrifice"?

5. What do you think Jesus is saying in the proverbs about cloth and wineskins (9:14-17)?

6. Compare the petition of the ruler in Matthew (9:18) with that in Mark (5:23).

7. How are Matthew 9:22 and 9:2 alike?

8. What is the difference in the cure of the woman with a hemorrhage in Matthew 9:20-23 and in Mark 5:25-29?

9. Review the narrative section of Book Two (8:1—9:34) and the ten miracles. Which of these miracles has the most meaning for you?

Lesson 10 (9:35—11:1).

This lesson is the discourse section of Book Two called the Missionary Sermon. It begins with the sending of the disciples and concludes with some sayings on discipleship.

1. Why do you think Jesus tells His disciples to stay away from Gentile territory in 10:5-6?

2. Compare 9:35-37 with 4:23-24. How do these sections differ?

3. Why does Matthew include verses 8-10? What is Christ talking about here in addition to poverty?

4. The term "sheep" is used in 9:36, 10:6, and 10:16. Who do you think the "sheep" are in each of these verses?

5. Jesus tells His disciples in 10:17-18 that they will suffer persecution for His sake. Do you think that this is a necessary thing? Could you be a good disciple without the necessity of suffering persecution? Give reasons for your answer.

6. Read Acts 4:8 and 13:9. What does 10:20 mean to you? Has the Spirit ever spoken in your heart?

7. *How* will he who endures to the end be saved (10:22)?

8. In 10:36, Jesus says a man's enemies will be members of his own family. Do Jesus' words have

any bearing on today's world, or do they merely show the conditions of His own time? Give reasons for your answer.

9. What does Jesus mean in verse 38 about taking up a cross? Do you think He is predicting His own passion, or is He warning His disciples that they will be treated as criminals, or what? Discuss.

Lesson 11 (11:2—11:30).

This lesson marks the beginning of Book Three on Controversy and Parables. The first part of this book is the narrative section on the incredulity and hostility of the Jews.

1. Read the following in Isaiah: 26:19, 29:18, 35:5, and 61:1. How do these statements compare with Jesus' words in Matthew 11:4-5?

2. Why do you think John sent his disciples to question Jesus?

3. What is your understanding of 11:16?

4. In 11:16-19, Jesus describes the Jews' disbelief in the Good News as a childish rejection of both Jesus and John. Why do you think the Jews rejected the Good News?

5. What conclusions can you draw about the success of Jesus' work in Galilee by His words in 11:20-24?

6. Verses 25-30 have a different tone from the rest of this chapter. How would you describe these verses?

7. Compare 11:28-30 with 7:14. How can you reconcile these statements? What do you think is meant by each?

8. What meaning does verse 30 have for you?

Lesson 12 (12:1 — 12:50).

This lesson is the last part of the narrative section in Book Three.

1. (Read the following as background for 12:1-8: Hos. 6:6; Is. 1:16-17, 29:13; and 1 Sam. 21:4.) What do you think Matthew is saying about Jesus' authority in the Sabbath controversy on plucking corn?

2. What does 12:7 mean in modern terms?

3. What are the implications of verses 6-8?

4. Compare 12:9-14 with Mark 3:1-6. How do these accounts differ?

5. Why do you think the Pharisees were angry over the Sabbath healing?

6. The accusation of the Pharisees (12:22-24) dismisses Jesus' miracles as magic acts rendered through the intercession of demons. How do you think this accusation affected the disciples? The crowds?

7. What does 12:30 say to you?

8. What do you think Jesus is saying in 12:46-50, considering the great emphasis the Jews placed on family ties?

Lesson 13 (13:1 — 13:32).

This lesson is the first part of the discourse section of Book Three and is concerned with the Parables of the Reign.

1. What do you think is the point of the Parable of the Sower (13:1-9)? Rewrite this parable choosing a setting other than one of sowing seed and farming.

2. What do you think is the special "something" the person in verse 12 has? What ingredient is Jesus saying is necessary in order to understand the parables?

3. Why do you think Jesus taught in parables?

4. The interpretation of the Parable of the Sower (13:18-23) is generally thought to have come from the early Church and not from Jesus Himself. Give a modern day interpretation of this parable.

5. Give an example of a situation similar to the Parable of the Sower in 13:24-30.

6. Using modern terms, compose a contrasting situation like the Parable of the Mustard Seed (13:31-32) to describe the beginnings of the Church.

7. Which of the parables in this lesson impresses you the most? Why?

Lesson 14 (13:33 — 13:52).

The discourse on the Parables of the Reign concludes with this lesson.

1. What does the Parable of the Leaven (13:33) say to you?

2. Compare Matthew 13:34-35 with Mark 4:10-12 and 4:33-34. How do these passages differ?

3. What does the explanation of the Parable of the Sower (13:36-43) say to you about tolerance and judgment?

4. Explain the Parable of the Treasure and the Pearl (13:44-46).

5. What does the Parable of the Net (13:47-50) mean to you? How is it different from the two preceding parables?

6. What overall picture of the kingdom do you get from the parables in chapter 13?

7. Which parable in chapter 13 has the most meaning for you? Give a reason for your answer.

Lesson 15 (13:53—14:36).

This lesson marks the beginning of Book Four: The Formation of the Disciples. The first part of the book is the narrative section concerning various episodes preceding the journey to Jerusalem.

1. Give an example from your own life to support the validity of Jesus' statement in 13:57.

2. Why do you think Jesus' townspeople had no faith in Him (13:58)?

3. What implications are there in Herod's statement about Jesus in 14:2, considering the fact that Herod was responsible for John's death?

4. Compare Matthew 14:3-12 with Mark 6:17-29. How do they differ?

5. 14:3-12 is a flashback concerning the death of John the Baptist. Why do you think John was imprisoned and killed?

6. What significance do Jesus' actions in 14:13 have for you? What meaning do you think John's death had for Jesus?

7. Why do you think all three synoptic gospels place the miracle of the feeding of the five thousand immediately after Jesus hears of the death of John?

8. What reason can you give for Jesus' statement to the apostles in 14:16?

9. What do you think the story of the feeding of the five thousand means?

10. What symbols can you identify in the story of Jesus walking on the water (14:22-23)?

Lesson 16 (15:1—16:12).

The narrative section of Book Four continues.

1. This chapter opens with another conflict story between Jesus and the Scribes and Pharisees. Why do you think Matthew includes this story . . . is he merely trying to relate events in Jesus' ministry, or does his story meet some need in the early Church? Discuss.

2. The controversy with the Pharisees is not one of the "spirit of the law" versus the "letter of the law" but about the tension between Pharisee tradition and the Law of God. What guidelines do you use in your own life to resolve conflicts of this sort?

3. Read Isaiah 29:13-14 (partially quoted in Mt. 15:8-9). Recall an incident from your own life that either illustrates Isaiah's words or Matthew's interpretation of them.

4. Peter asks for an explanation of the parable or saying in 15:15. Do you think Peter really needed to have this simple saying explained, or has Matthew another motive for including this passage? Why do you think it was included?

5. Compare Matthew 14:13-21 with Matthew 15:32-39. List the differences in these versions of what was probably the same event. Considering Matthew's use of symbolic objects and events, give a reason for the differences in these stories. Why do you think the feeding of the four thousand was included?

6. Compare Matthew 16:1-4 with Matthew 12:38-41. Matthew says (12:40) that the sign of Jonah symbolizes Christ's resurrection. What do you think are the implications of the Pharisees asking for a sign at this stage of Jesus' career?

7. If you have ever asked for a sign from God, share the experience with the others in your group.

8. How do the versions of the story of the leaven (Mt. 16:5-12 and Mk. 8:14-21) differ? Discuss.

Lesson 17 (16:13—17:27).

This is the conclusion of the narrative section of Book Four.

1. Compare Matthew 16:13-23 with Mark 8:27-30. Discuss the differences in these stories.

2. What is your own interpretation of Matthew 16:17-19?

3. What is the cross that you carry to follow Jesus?

4. What do you think the transfiguration (17:1-8) meant to Peter, James, and John?

5. Discuss the use of symbols in the story of the transfiguration in light of the Old Testament: the mountain, shining face, white garments, Moses and Elijah, bright cloud. (See Ex. 19:3, 16; 33:20; and 34:29-30.)

6. Read Mark 9:2-32. Compare these stories with Matthew 17:1-23. List the main differences in these versions. How can you account for these differences, especially as they refer to the characters of the apostles?

7. What does the story of the Temple Tax mean to you? What do you think it meant to the early Church?

Lesson 18 (18:1—18:35).

This lesson is on Book Four's discourse: The Sermon on the Church. It is concerned with the relationships of the Church members toward each other.

1. What do you think Matthew is trying to tell us about Christian leadership in 18:1-5?

2. What do you think Jesus means by verse 3 . . . becoming "like little children"?

3. How do you think you are living up to the ideals set forth in 18:1-5 in your own parish community?

4. What does the section (18:6-9) say to you personally? Discuss the figurative nature of the statements here. How much of this is literary device, and how much is real and not figurative?

5. What point is Matthew making with the story of the Shepherd and the Lost Sheep (18:10-14), especially as it concerns leadership in the Church? Compare this story with Luke 15:3-7 for another outlook to the same story.

6. Discuss the ideals of Christian community contained in 18:15-20, as it concerns fraternal correction (15-16), excommunication (17), decisions of the Church assembly (18) and formation of the assembly (19-20). Include a comparison of these passages with your own experience of the Church you know today.

7. What meaning does the story of the Unforgiving Servant (18:21-25) have for you? Paraphrase it in more modern terms.

Lesson 19 (19:1—20:28).

This lesson marks the beginning of Book Five, and includes the beginning of the narrative: The Journey to Jerusalem and What Happened There.

1. Compare Matthew 5:31-32 with Matthew 19:5-9. How can you reconcile these statements with Jesus' claim that he didn't come to destroy the Law, but to fulfill it?

2. Explain your understanding of 19:10-12 as it relates to celibacy.

3. Compare Matthew 19:16-30 with Mark 10:17-31, listing the differences. Why do you think the man did not choose to follow Jesus?

4. Why does wealth seem to be such a barrier to the kingdom?

5. How does verse 26 offer hope to the rich?

6. Discuss your own understanding of the Parable of the Laborers in the Vineyard. How is your interpretation affected by the "position" of this parable between the promise that the twelve apostles would occupy thrones (19:28) and the sons of Zebedee asking about their place in the kingdom (20:21)?

7. Compare the third prediction of the passion (20:17-19) with the first (16:21) and the second (17:22-23).

8. Give an example of a person, from your own experience, who could be described by the passage 20:26-28.

Lesson 20 (20:29—21:27).

A continuation of the narrative section of Book Five.

1. What do you think is the significance of the story of the two blind men (20:29-34) considering the following: type of cure, position in story just before the entry into Jerusalem, the way the blind men address Jesus?

2. Read Isaiah 62:11 and Zechariah 9:9. Compare Matthew 21:1-9 with Mark 11:1-11. What do you find meaningful about the differences?

3. In the story of the expulsion from the temple (21:13) Jesus quotes from Isaiah 56:7 and Jeremiah 7:1, and He uses ideas from Psalm 8:2 and Wisdom 10:21 (in 21:16). What is Jesus saying about His authority by these words, and by His actions: driving out the money changers, the cures?

4. Read Isaiah 5:2, 7; Jeremiah 8:13; and Hosea 9:16 as background. What do you think the fig tree in Matthew 21:18-19 symbolizes?

5. In 21:21 and 22, Jesus gives us two sayings on faith. Which of these sayings has the most meaning for you? Why?

6. Why do you think the priests and elders questioned Jesus' authority?

7. What criterion do you use for recognizing authority?

8. What is there about this story (21:23-27) that points out the failure of Israel implied in the story of the fig tree?

Lesson 21 (21:28—22:46).

A continuation of the narrative section of Book Five, this lesson includes three parables and four controversy stories.

1. Discuss your understanding of the Parable of the Two Sons (21:28-32). How can you apply this parable today?

2. Explain the allegorical features of the Parable of the Wicked Husbandmen (21:33-46) as it refers to Jesus' time.

3. Discuss the allegory of the wedding feast (22:1-10). Compare the point of this parable with the first two parables in this lesson.

4. Compare the Parable of the Wedding Garment (22:11-13) with that of the Sower (13:36-43) and the Net (13:47-50). What point is Jesus making with these parables?

5. What is your understanding of Christ's words in 22:21? What belongs to "Caesar" today, and what belongs to God?

6. What is Jesus saying about life after death in the controversy story in 22:23-33?

7. Jesus' answer to the Sadducees in the controversy over the greatest commandment (22:34-40) cites Deuteronomy 6:5 and Leviticus 19:18, and gives both laws equal value, something the Pharisees did not do. In light of this, what is your understanding of Christ's words in 22:40? How do you "love" God?

8. Jesus demonstrates in His question about David that the Pharisees are not competent religious leaders since they cannot interpret a messianic text. What answer should the Pharisees have given to Jesus' question?

Lesson 22 (23:1—24:31).

This lesson consists of the last part of the narrative section of Book Five concerning Jesus' invectives against the Scribes and Pharisees, and the beginning of the Discourse: The Eschatological Sermon.

1. In 23:1-7, Jesus condemns the religious hypocrisy and vanity of the Scribes and Pharisees in contrast to their rigorous interpretation of the law.

Discuss these verses in light of present devotional practices, giving specific examples from your own experience.

2. Matthew 18:15, 20:24-28, and 23:11-12 present similar ideas on humility. Discuss your understanding of the symbols of "little child" and "servant" as they apply to your own conduct as a Christian.

3. Read the seven "woes" in 23:13 to 23:36. Select the "woe" that has the most meaning for you, and try to express it in terms of modern day experience. (Such as "woe" No. 4: "Alas for you, hypocrites, who religiously fill your Lenten mite box with daily pennies, and neglect your lonely neighbor waiting in vain for a friendly visit from you.")

4. Compare Matthew 24:1-31 with Mark 13:1-27. Both of these accounts include a prediction, as well as description, of the destruction of Jerusalem in 70 A.D. What evidence can you find that shows that Matthew was written after 70 A.D. and Mark was written before?

5. Do you think that 24:9-14 is only a description of the persecution of the early Christian Church, or can it also be referring to the fate of the Christian today? Give a reason for your answer.

6. What meaning does the apocalyptical description of the Parousia (24:29-31) have for you personally? How are you preparing for the coming of the Son?

Lesson 23 (24:32—25:46).

This lesson, the conclusion of the Eschatological

Discourse, includes sayings on the Parousia and three parables on the final judgment.

1. The Parable of the Fig Tree (24:32-33) in referring to spring and budding shoots, seems to suggest an attitude of hope. How does this interpretation fit in with your own idea of the parousia?

2. The three sayings on the parousia echo similar passages: 24:34 and 16:28, 24:35 and 5:18, and 24:36 and Acts 1:7. What point do you think the third saying (24:36) is making about the human nature of Jesus?

3. What meaning does the exhortation to vigilance in 24:37-41 have for you?

4. What do you think the Story of the Prudent Householder (24:42-44) says about the parousia?

5. Do you think that the Parable of the Faithful and Prudent Servant refers to apostolic functions in the Church (see 1 Cor. 4:1-3) or does it express the eschatological lot common to all Christians?

6. Rephrase the Parable of the Wise and Foolish Virgins in modern terms, keeping in mind the point of the story. Discuss the implications of 25:11 in light of 7:21.

7. What is the point of the Parable of the Talents?

8. What does Matthew's picture of the "weeping and gnashing of teeth" (25:30) symbolize for you? (See also 8:12, 13:42, 13:50, 22:13, and 24:51.)

9. How can you reconcile these facts: Jesus says that the law is, "Love God, and your neighbor as yourself" yet in the parabolic story of the Last Judgment (25:31-46)He says that we will be judged on love of neighbor, and does not mention our duty to God.

Lesson 24 (26:1—26:75).

This lesson is the beginning of the passion narrative.

1. What effect do you think Jesus' predictions in 26:2 and 26:11 had on the apostles? Put yourself in place of one of them and decide how you would have reacted.

2. Why do you think Judas wanted to betray Jesus (26:14-16)?

3. Do you think Matthew means us to think Judas' statement in 26:25 is sheer hypocrisy, or that perhaps he hasn't decided whether or not to betray Jesus?

4. Read 1 Corinthians 11:23-25 and Jeremiah 31:31-34. Discuss the Eucharist as a commemoration of the new covenant, comparing it to the old covenant meal of the Passover.

5. Compare Peter's reaction to Jesus' prediction of his denial in 26:30-35 to your own confidence before a fall.

6. What effect does reading Hebrews 5:7-10 and Matthew 26:36-46 about the anguish of Jesus have on you?

7. What does the fact that the chief priests and elders sent the crowd at night to arrest Jesus (26:47-56) say about public sentiment toward Jesus?

8. What do you think was the reason for Peter's denial of Christ in 26:69-75—fear of being involved, pride, cowardice???

Lesson 25 (27:1—27:56).

The passion narrative continues.

1. After reading Zechariah 11:12-13 and Exodus

21:32, what meaning do you attach to the thirty pieces of silver (26:15)? What do they mean to Judas in 27:5?

2. Compare the Sanhedrin's charge of blasphemy because Christ claimed divinity (26:64) with the accusation made before Pilate (27:11). How can you explain this difference?

3. Pilate thought that the chief priests and elders delivered Jesus to him out of jealousy (27:18). What do you think?

4. Compare 26:67-68 with 27:27-31. How do you feel about Jesus after reading these sections?

5. Read Psalm 22 which Christ prays in 27:46. Compare Matthew 27:36 with Psalm 22:18 and Matthew 27:43 with Psalm 22:8. What do you think Christ meant by His words in 27:46? What do they mean to you personally?

6. Compare 27:34 with Psalm 69:22, 27:45 with Amos 8:9 and Jeremiah 4:23, 27:51, with Hebrews 10:19-20, 27:52, with Jeremiah 4:24, 27:52-53, with Isaiah 26:19, and 27:52-55, with Ezekial 37:12-13, and Daniel 12:2. What do you think is significant about the events in 27:45-53?

7. What reasons can you give for the statement of the centurion in 27:54?

Lesson 26 (27:57—28:20).

The concluding verses of the passion narrative and the final section of the Gospel of Matthew: The Resurrection Narrative.

1. Compare Matthew 27:57-61 with Mark 15:42-47. How do these accounts differ?

2. Cite facts given by Matthew in 27:59—28:10 that show that the resurrection actually occurred.

3. What does the empty tomb in 28:1-10 symbolize for you?

4. Why do you think Matthew included the incidents mentioned in 27:62-66 and 28:11-15?

5. Enumerate the "orders" given by Jesus to the apostles in 28:16-20. What significance does the Apostolic Commission have for Christians today?

6. What meaning does the last sentence of Matthew's Gospel have for you?

7. What has impressed you the most in reading and studying the Gospel of Matthew?

6

Ephesians

Lesson 1 (1:1—2:10).

1. What are the spiritual blessings you see in Ephesians 1:1-14 for which you would praise God?

2. The phrase "in Christ" or "in Him" is used many times in Ephesians. What is Paul telling us about being "in Christ"? What significance does this phrase have for you?

3. What does Ephesians 1:18-19 say and mean to you? How have you seen this "immeasurable greatness of His power in us who believe" in your own life?

4. What does the phrase "uniting all things in Christ" (1:10) mean to you?

   A. How do you relate this to your life experience?

   B. How does the idea of "the completion of Him who fills us all" (1:23) relate to this?

5. In 2:4-10 there are a number of references to the word "grace" or "favor." What is the real meaning that Paul is trying to bring out here? What is your personal understanding of "grace"?

Challenge Question:

6. We are reminded in 2:1-6 that whatever our call to conversion has been that we were once dead by reason of our sins. What value can remembering the evil from which you were called have in your present life? What meaning can reinterpreting your conversion moments have for you?

Lesson 2 (2:11—3:21).

1. Read Ephesians 2:11-16. The writer says that at one time all people, especially the Gentiles, had no hope, but are now made new men, reconciled to God into one body through the blood of Christ. Read Hebrews 9 and share any new insights you have gained into the meaning of the new covenant that Christ sealed with His blood.

2. In this letter to the Ephesians Paul writes of unity between Christian Jews and Gentiles. What do you believe are the principal problems facing Christian unity today? Discuss steps we can take to promote this ideal.

3. In 3:2-9, Paul speaks of his teaching mission. What is the "mystery" which has been hidden in God until Paul's preaching mission revealed it?

4. It is expressed in 2:8-9 and again in 3:7-13 that by the gift of God's grace we have been made ministers.

    A. Do these lines indicate what we are to do with this gift?

    B. How can we maintain an openness to how God wants us to devote ourselves to the good deeds He has designed for us?

5. Read Paul's prayer (3:14-21) meditatively. Re-

flect on the phrase, "You are filled with the utter fullness of God." Share your immediate response with the group.

Lesson 3 (4:1—5:20).

1. Read 4:1-6. Verse 4:1 tells us we are to live a life worthy of our calling. What are some of the ways in which we can accomplish this?

2. Paul refers to grace as gifts in 4:7-16. How does grace affect the unity of the body of Christ?

3. According to Paul, Christ is the head of His body, giving it its unity, its growth in truth and love (4:14-16). Share what you think are the qualities of a "head" (a leader, a president, etc.) that give unity, growth, truth, and love to a "body" (a group, etc.).

4. In 4:17-24, Paul tells us we must put off the old self and clothe ourselves with Christ. Use Colossians 3:10-17 to show how we can begin to fashion our new selves into the image of God.

5. Paul (4:25-32) lists several vices which Christians should be particularly careful to avoid. Explain which of these strikes you as the most difficult to handle.

6. In 5:1-7, Paul tells us to imitate God and cautions us about fornication, impurity, and promiscuity. In today's world with mass media how can we guide our children to avoid these pitfalls and remain true children of God?

Challenge Questions:

7. In Ephesians 5:8-20, walking as a child of light and testing what is well pleasing to God represents a life-long process to which each Christian is called.

A. Discuss the kinds of feelings this awakens within you.

B. What are the supports in your life right now whereby this process is encouraged within you?

8. The singing and making melody in your hearts to the Lord (5:19-20) speak of a deep Christian joy. Share some experience of your own when you were able to realize this kind of joy.

Lesson 4 (5:21—6:24).

1. Read 5:21-26. Paul sees in a marital relationship a reflection and a symbol of the relationship between Christ and the Church.

A. Do you feel submitting destroys a woman's freedom? Give your reasons why or why not.

B. How does a Christian who is in sympathy with the current beliefs and principles of women's rights explain what is really meant in 5:21-26?

2. In 5:31-32 Paul explains that man and woman united in marriage is the same as the union of Christ and us in the Church. How do you personally view this mystery? What are its implications?

3. What does 6:1-4 tell us about family relationships today?

4. In 6:5-8, Paul does not condone slavery, but he tells slaves to make their condition supernatural. When you feel "enslaved," how can you give your "service with good will as to the Lord" (6:7)?

5. "Whatever good each does, the same he will receive back from the Lord" (6:8). In what way do you experience this?

Challenge Question:

6. List the qualities or virtues that Paul encourages us to put on in the practice of our faith (6:10-17).

- A. Comment on those qualities which seem most a part of your Christian life today.
- B. Discuss which qualities you think are essential to your readiness and zeal in carrying the Good News to others.
- C. This putting on of the armor can only have deep meaning if it is followed by what Paul speaks of in 6:18-20. What part do prayer and perseverance in prayer have to do with your sharing in the body of Christ?

7

Corinthians

Lesson 1 (1:1—2:5).

1. How would you compare Paul's introduction (1:1-9) to a father's concern for his children?

2. In 1:10-16, Paul exhorts us to be firmly joined in unity of mind and thought. How do you put this into practice in your life?

3. In 1:18, Paul divides mankind into two classes. Which class do you place yourself in and why do you feel you are in that class?

4. Taking Paul's advice to "consider your own call," (1:26-31), reflect in yourself to see the truth of what he said. Share one or two instances in your experience to give glory to God.

5. Reflect and share how you are an example like Paul of the "weakness" of the Gospel in your life of witness (2:1-5).

Lesson 2 (2:6—4:21).

1. In 2:6 the evangelist speaks of having wisdom to offer those who have reached maturity. What is the wisdom of which he speaks? See also Colossians 2:20-23 and Hebrews 5:14.

2. What message does Paul have for us in 3:1-4?

3. There are both support and responsibilities contained in 3:16-17.

    A. What supports do you sense God has given you to maintain the foundation He has established. See also 2 Corinthians 6:16 and Ephesians 2:20-22.

    B. What responsibilities are ours—socially, physically, mentally, and spiritually?

4. In 3:18—4:5, we are called to be servants, stewards of the Lord. What does this tell us about our abilities to judge? Who can judge us?

5. In 4:8-13, how does Paul reveal his absolute commitment to Christ?

6. What does Paul mean when he says (4:20) "The Kingdom of God is not just words, it is power"? (Also see 2:4.)

Lesson 3 (5:1 — 6:20).

    1.A. Search your own experience and see if there are any examples of "old yeast" which have spoiled something good and healthy. (Refer to 5:6-8.)

    B. Compare the man in 5:1 to the old yeast and its effects on the dough and the community.

2. In 6:7, Paul is saying to suffer a little injustice. What could this possibly do? Share your reactions to this Christian advice. (See Lk. 6:27-30.)

3. Some Corinthians were invoking Christian liberty to justify serious violations of morality. What do you think Paul was talking about when he said, "for me there are no forbidden things" (6:12)? (See also Rom. 14:14-20 and 1 Cor. 10:23.)

4. There were disorders in the Corinthian church that Paul had to deal with and defend the faith and his role as an apostle. Corinth was a cosmopolitan city steeped with the Greek spirit of independence, with the intellectual pride of the Greek mind and its search for novelty and controversy. How would you apply Paul's defense of the faith and the role of an apostle in our time and area?

5. In chapters 5 and 6, Paul deals with sexual disorders and appeals to the civil courts which Paul considers unjust. What would Paul find changed in our day and how do you think he would deal with the same "problems"?

Lesson 4 (7:1—7:40).

1. Read 7:3-5. What does this say to you about the marriage relationship?

2. In 7:17-24, Paul stresses the importance of being yourself, but it is most important to become the "slave of the Lord." Share your views on Paul's seemingly contradictory ideas about becoming really free through knowing Christ and becoming really free by being His slave.

3. Does Paul's message (7:25-31) have meaning for you today? Defend your answer.

4. Paul says in 7:33 that "man and wife are torn in two ways"—in pleasing each other and in serving God. How do you handle this problem in your daily life?

Lesson 5 (8:1—9:27).

1. In principle Paul is saying in 8:1-6 that enlightened Christians are completely free to de-

cide for themselves. Do you as a Christian have as much difficulty in applying this principle today in the reality in which you live? If so, share examples.

2. "Take care lest perhaps this right of yours become a stumbling block to the weak" (8:9). Reflect and share your ideas or feelings on how you would react to forego your liberty, even if you are right, to prevent any harm to the conscience of another.

3. In your own words, what is Paul telling the Corinthians about his rank or authority as an apostle? Refer to chapter 9.

4. Inclination and duty seemed to have found a happy meeting point in Paul and his preaching the message of deliverance (9:16-18). Try to remember and share an incident in your own life when inclination and duty have coincided.

5. What kind of person does Paul describe himself to be in 9:19-23? What type of person does that remind you of today?

6. To what is Paul referring in 9:24-27 in the life of a Christian?

Lesson 6 (10:1 — 11:34).

1. "You can trust God not to let you be tried beyond your strength, and with any trial He will give you a way out of it and the strength to bear it" (10:13). (See also Eccles. [Sirach] 15:11-20, 1 Cor. 1:9, Jas. 1:3-14, and Mt. 6:13 and 26:41.) How do you use or misuse this special gift God gives you?

2. The subject of food sacrificed to idols is once again referred to in 10:14-22. By using an analogy Paul is warning the Corinthians. Share with the group your understanding of this analogy and

whether it has meaning for you now. Refer to 2 Corinthians 6:14-16.

3. Compare 10:23—11:1 with what the Church is teaching today on moral responsibility.

4. Discuss 11:2-16. Good luck!

5. Refer to 11:17-22. Paul speaks very strongly about unity in a community, or else the meal is not the *Lord's Supper*. In celebrating the Eucharist, how can you reconcile the differences in the community within a typical parish today?

Lesson 7 (12:1—12:30).

1. Paul says in 12:3, "And no one can say Jesus is Lord, except in the Holy Spirit." How do you feel the Holy Spirit inspires us to share this gift?

2. In 12:4-11, Paul tells us about the special gifts bestowed by the Spirit. Which of these gifts is most meaningful to you? Why?

3. Paul uses the analogy of the human body to bring out our unity with Christ. Meditate on 12:12-13 and Romans 12:4-5. Share your understanding of this analogy and what it means to you personally.

4. In 12:14-21, Paul says each member of Christ's mystical body can perform only its own function, but all are necessary. How do the members "communicate" with each other to preserve unity in the body? Share your reflections.

5. ". . . but that all the members may be concerned for one another" (12:25). This verse contains one of the key elements of "Christian community." Reflect upon the various communities to

which you belong (social, religious, business, educational, etc.). Where is the evidence of concern to be found?

6. In 12:27-30, what do you think were Paul's intentions in separating the roles of the Church? In the name of unity, how does his differentiation of roles avoid a "pecking order" in the hierarchical structure of the Church?

Lesson 8 (12:31 — 14:40).

1. In 12:31, Paul states that we should "set our hearts on the greater gifts."
   A. Define your concept of the greater gift.
   B. From your experience share as many ways as you can in which you set your heart on the greater gifts.

2. In 13:4-7, Paul paints a portrait of fraternal love—what it does and what it refuses to do. Do you feel people are afraid to "love"? Explain.

3. In 13:13, Paul says: "There are three things that last: faith, hope, and love; and the greatest of these is love." Share how each of these graces fits and works in your life.

4. We know that the gift of love is the greatest of the spiritual gifts. However, 14:1 speaks of the gift of prophecy. What is your understanding of this gift? How is it to be used?

5. Read 14:6-9. What experience do you have of "speaking to the empty air"?

6. (14:20-25) If the gift of prophecy and the ability to be a witness to one's faith are one and the same:

A. What do you think would be the effect upon a non-believer to experience a person with the gift of prophecy?
B. Search deeply within yourself. How have you been made aware of this gift in others and especially in yourself?

7. In 14:34-35, Paul has some comments to make about women that are considered chauvinistic in today's language. However, he seems to justify his reasoning by the law, to which he elsewhere refers as a means rather than an absolute end (2 Cor. 3:6). How would Paul's ideas be received today?

Lesson 9 (15:1 — 15:58).

1. Read 15:1-11. Paul enumerates witnesses to the resurrection:
A. Why do you feel this was necessary?
B. How do we still witness Christ's resurrection today?

2. Accepting the resurrection of Christ gives us victory over death. How does this freedom help you in your life (15:12-19)?

3. All that are by faith united to Christ are by His resurrection assured of their own (15:22-23). What do you think is intended by "*All of them in their proper order*"?

4. In 15:31 Paul says, "I face death every day." Do you feel it is a risk to stand up for what you believe? If so, share your experience.

5. In 15:36 can be heard an echo of Jesus' saying in John's Gospel (12:24), "Unless the grain of wheat falls into the ground and dies, it remains alone. But

if it dies, it brings forth much fruit." Reflect and share what you think Jesus and Paul are telling you about your "grain of wheat."

6. Read 15:54-58. The phrase, "By His resurrection Christ conquered death for us" is often cited. What is your understanding of this in terms of the immortality of your physical body?

Lesson 10 (16:1 — 16:24).
(Review 1:1 — 16:24)

1. Read 16:1-9. How does Paul seem like a friend and close member of the community?

2. In 16:23-24, Paul once again expresses his love for the people of Corinth despite all their defects. How would you compare Paul's signature to a parent's signature in a letter to one of his adult children?

3. From the first four chapters of 1 Corinthians, pick your favorite passage and share. Why is it special to you?

4. What do you think of Paul's attitude toward this world in 7:29-31? Refer to 2 Corinthians 4:7-15 and 6:1-18 for help.

5. Paul asks: "Am I not free? Am I not an apostle? Have I not seen Jesus our Lord? Are not you my work in the Lord" (9:12)?

   A. How did Paul answer these questions (use 9:12)?

   B. How do you answer these questions for yourself?

6. "I chastise my body and bring it into subjection, lest perhaps after preaching to others I myself should be rejected" (9:27). Share your ideas and

attitudes on chastisement, mortification or discipline of the body to ensure having a share in the salvation which the Gospel affords.

7. Read 13:4-7, substituting your name in the place of "Love."

    A. Meditate on these verses. If you dare, share your experiences.

    B. Love is the greatest gift from God and all other gifts are given in love. Share with us the special gifts you may have received during your study of Paul's letter to the Corinthians.

8

The First and Second Letters of Peter

Lesson 1 (1 Peter 1:1—1:25).

1. Some scholars claim that much of the content of the first letter of Peter is taken from early baptismal instructions. What baptismal symbolism and meaning can you find in 1 Peter 1:1-6?

2. Read 1:6-9. Share about a time in your life when you came to meet the person of Jesus in a period of trial. Through this experience how was your faith in Him strengthened to bring great cause for rejoicing?

3. The Jewish prophets lived in an era before Christ, yet Peter writes that the Spirit of Christ was in them (1:10-11). What is your understanding of Peter's statement? (Read also Jn. 1:1-5 and 1 Pet. 1:20.)

4. 1:16 says, "Be holy, for I am holy." What does being holy mean to you? How do you go about achieving this state of being holy?

5. Read 1:17-21. Peter points out that it is because of Christ's death and resurrection that we have cause for faith and hope in God. Reflect on:

A. Whether your own life is God-centered.

B. Your own death and resurrection.

6. The people of Peter's time held a belief that the spoken word was powerful and could create reality. The power of the word was determined by the authority of the speaker and the spoken word of God was endowed with immeasurable power. Read 1:22-25 and share your thoughts on:

A. The creative power of God's spoken word in your life.

B. Your power as the "speaker" of God's word.

Challenge Question:

Chapter 1 of 1 Peter seems to be a sermon on faith, leading the readers to elect the path of holiness of Jesus.

A. How did you react to the chapter?

B. What would you emphasize or change to lead modern readers to elect Jesus' path to holiness?

Lesson 2 (1 Peter 2:1—3:7).

1. Read 2:1-3. Peter calls the disciples to *be* who they really *are* in their new life. What ingredients, do you think, comprise the spiritual milk that true disciples would naturally crave as "newborns"?

2. In 1 Peter 2:4-10 Peter reminds the disciples that they were chosen by God, along with Jesus as the cornerstone, to be living stones in making a spiritual house.

A. Share how Christ is the cornerstone in your life.

B. What responsibility accompanies the

privilege of sharing in "the holy priest-hood"?

3. Read 2:11-12. Recall in your life a time when you were a source of Christian inspiration helping another to respond to God's visitation and call. Recall an experience in your life when another's Christian example and inspiration were for you an opening of awareness to God's visitation and call.

4. 2:16 calls Christians to live as free men. Using Galatians 5:13 and James 1:25, how can we apply these principles to our Christian lives today?

5. If you should feel oppressed, how would you react to someone giving you the advice in 2:18-20? See also Paul's comments in Ephesians 6:5-8.

6. Read 2:21-25, Matthew 5:38-48 and 16:24-28. In these verses are some of the most fundamental teachings of Jesus. Share what meaning these have for you.

7. Read 3:1-7. What duties and qualities of married life does this passage outline? How do the relationships in your home compare with them? (See also Eph. 5:21-28.)

Lesson 3 (1 Peter 3:8—5:14).

1. In 3:8-12, characteristics of Christian charity are mentioned. Ponder the relationships active in your life in the light of this passage. Share your insights.

2. Read 3:13-19. Christ was the living example of the body being put to death and the spirit raised to life. How do you think this dying and rising takes place in our daily lives?

3. In 4:1-6, what is Peter telling his readers

about the suffering Christ in relation to their own lives? How does this apply to us today?

4. In the often-quoted passage from 1 Peter 4:7-11, we are encouraged to have certain virtues.

    A. Which one of these directives is most important in your experiences?

    B. Share which one you need to foster in your life.

5. Why should a Christian not be surprised at being persecuted (4:12)? Share how you are or are not persecuted today for being a Christian. Share what ways you deal with "persecution" as a Christian.

6. 5:1-11 outlines the delicate balance and interdependence between the leaders and the members of the Christian community. How could you better fulfill your vocation to help achieve this relationship within your Christian community?

Lesson 4 (2 Peter 1:1—2:3).

1. What does it mean to you to share in the divine nature as promised in 1:4?

2. In 1:5-11, Peter tells us about the progressive steps we should take to lead a Christian life. (Read also 1 Jn. 2:15 and Gal. 5:22.) Tell how the Spirit helps you along this path.

3. In 1:12-15, Peter attempts to fulfill his mission with the realization of his own approaching death. Is the way you are living based on the assumption that you have many more years to live? Would you live differently if you had a very short time left to live?

4. Read 1:19 and reflect upon and share experi-

ences when you recognized Jesus as your "lamp shining in a dark place."

  5. Meditate on 1:20-21. Share your feelings on:
     A. How the Holy Spirit speaks through humankind.
     B. Who can interpret prophecy?
     C. How we can receive prophecy as truth.
  6. In chapter 2, Peter refers to false prophets who have been plaguing the Christian community. (Read Deut. 13:2-6, Mt. 24:23-24, and Jude 4.)
     A. What was the resulting danger of these false prophets which caused Peter so much concern?
     B. How do we recognize false prophets and are they a threat today?

Lesson 5 (2 Peter 2:4—3:18).

  1. The message of 2:4-10a is not so much one of divine vengeance as one of God's mercy. How do you experience the forgiveness and mercy of God in your life through others, through the Church, in daily happenings?
  2. In 2:15-16, the author refers to an Old Testament false prophet type, Balaam (Num. 22-24). 2 Peter 2:10-16 tells of the arrogance of the false prophets. Read both Scripture passages and share your thoughts.
  3. Are we as Christians strongly influenced by the society we live in? Do you believe the moral climate you live in affects your spiritual life? (Read 2:17-22.)
  4. Read 3:1-4. Many people in the world do not believe in or expect the parousia (the second com-

ing of Christ). What is your understanding of the second coming? What are you doing to prepare for it?

5. In 3:5-13, how did the author refute those who scoffed that the second coming would never take place? How did he answer those who were disturbed by the delay in the second coming? How is it possible to hasten the coming?

6. In 3:14, the author advises us to be free of sin and "at peace" in the sight of God while waiting for the second coming. What is this "peace" and how do we keep it?

Challenge Question:

Recall what passages most touched you from 1 Peter and from 2 Peter. Compare them and share your conclusions.

9

The Letter of Paul
to the Romans

Lesson 1 (1:1—3:20).

1. Read 1:17. What does this verse say to you?
How does faith lead to faith? How does the upright
man find life through faith?

2. Read 1:18-32. This passage says that we all
have, as the pagans had, a choice in knowing God
and then acting upon this knowledge. What does
"knowing God" mean to you? How do you act upon
it?

3. Comment on the ideas related to law as Paul
explored them in 2:12-16. How do these ideas apply
to you today?

4. In 2:25-29, what does Paul's statement on
being a Jew tell you about his growth as a Christian
following his persecution of the early Church?

5. What are the main points in the first eight
verses of Romans, chapter 3? What significance do
they have for you today?

6. In 3:19-20, Paul sums up how he sees the
purpose of the law. What is its purpose? What
more, if anything, is needed for salvation besides
knowledge of the law?

Paul expresses in the first chapters of Romans the inadequacies of paganism and Judaism to provide for salvation (Rom. 1:1—3:20). He lists the sins blighting life. Share what you think blights life and blocks salvation in your world.

Lesson 2 (3:21—5:11).

1. In 3:21-26, Paul reveals God's justice to us. What does Paul mean by God's justice? How can we avail ourselves of this justice?

2. What do you think were the opinions of Paul and Jesus on the value of the Jewish law as expressed in Romans, chapter 3 and in Matthew 5:17-20? How are they in agreement?

3. God's plan calls for faith rather than obedience to a legal system (4:13-17). What does this passage tell us about law and promise?

4. In chapter 4, what is Paul trying to point out by giving Abraham's example of faith? What meaning does it have for us today?

5. What kind of hope and appreciation are stirred up in you as you read 5:1-11?

Challenge Question:
In 3:21—4:25, Paul shows that the object of our faith is a personal relationship with Jesus Christ as Savior in our lives. Share how Jesus Christ's saving work in your life shows your faith relationship with Him (as Paul points out in Abraham's faith).

Lesson 3 (5:12—7:25).

1. What is the gift God gives all men according to

Romans 5:12-21? How do you feel about accepting this gift?

2. In 6:1-11, Paul tells us about baptism and its implications. How does baptism help to unite us with Christ? How does baptism continue to help through our lifetime?

3. Why do you believe Paul thought sin could not dominate your life if you lived by grace instead of by law (6:14)?

4. Compare the two contrasting ways of life and their effects presented by Paul in 6:15-23.

5. Read 7:1-13. Paul seems to identify law with sin and then law with good. What is he telling us about the function of the law?

6. In 7:14-24, Paul described the war going on in carnal man who lives without Christ. (Read 1 Cor. 10:13 and 1 Jn. 2:16-17.) Share your insights and comfort from these readings.

Challenge Question:

Christians believe that life comes from one man, Jesus Christ. How do we justify union with Jesus for those who do not know of Jesus' existence but do good and the Christians who are in union with Jesus but do not do what they profess?

Lesson 4 (8:1 — 10:4).

1. What is the "life" or "death" choice we have according to 8:12-14? What does it mean to you to live by the spirit? (Use Gal. 5:22-25 as further reference.)

2. Are there times and places that you cry out "Abba" (translated "daddy" or "papa")?

3. If we must endure with hope as Paul states in

8:22-27, where is our guarantee of salvation? What do 2 Corinthians 5:6-8, Hebrews 11:1, and Romans 5:1-11 say about this question?

4. Read Romans 8:31-39. Look into your own life. What obstacles do you find that keep you from responding more fully to the infinite love of God through Christ? What can you do to overcome them?

5. Paul refers to Pharoah in Romans 9:17-18. If man's hardness of heart becomes part of God's design, then how can man be accused of not doing the will of God? How does this allow for our free choice?

6. In chapter 9, what do you think Paul was feeling about the Jews treating Christ as though He were simply an obstacle in their course? Share how you experience the same thing happening today.

Challenge Question:

In chapter 8, Paul describes the spirit of one who surrenders to Jesus through living faith. Share what aspect of the spirit's leading was important to you in the reading of this chapter.

Lesson 5 (10:5—11:36).

1. Read 10:5-13. What do you think is the difference between the justice that comes from the observance of the law and the justice that comes from faith?

2. Paul explains that the people cannot come to believe in Jesus Christ unless someone is sent to bring the Good News (10:14). What obligation is implied for us in this verse? List several practical

steps that lay people could take to satisfy Paul's condition.

3. Paul wants to make it clear that salvation comes through God's mercy and not from personal merit. How does he express this in 11:1-10?

4. Why is Paul, a Jew, proud of his mission to preach to the Gentiles? How did his deep love for his own people show in Romans 11:11-15?

5. Romans 11:21-32 refers to the remnant of Israel. Paul tells of the good which has come about while Israel has been blind and also why the remnant will be saved. Share:

   A. Your understanding of the remnant of Israel.
   B. What good has come about from their disbelief.
   C. Why they will be saved.

Challenge Questions:

1. The theme of this epistle is stated in 1:16-17 and in 11:30-36. Express in your own words the meaning of either of these passages.

2. The theme of salvation is the whole import of Paul's teaching in chapter 11.

   A. Using your own thoughts and experiences, discuss what salvation is to you.
   B. Discuss some of the aspects of salvation which Paul emphasizes in Romans using any of the following: sin and death, justice and eternal life, hope, union with Christ, law, nature, gift, etc.
   C. Compare your own thoughts with what Paul was expressing.

Lesson 6 (12:1 — 15:13).

1. Read chapter 12. Meditate on the meaning of presenting your body as a sacrifice, living, holy, and pleasing to God. Share:
   A. How do you think this willingness to serve God could transform your life?
   B. Explain how chapter 12 is encompassed by verses 1 and 2.

2. Romans 13:1-7 tells us about our obligations toward all forms of government. Why do you think Paul thought it necessary to point out this fact?

3. Read Matthew 22:34-40 and compare it with Romans 13:8-10. How are Paul's and Jesus' teachings similar on the doctrine of the greatest commandments?

4. In chapter 14, Paul states that everyone should follow his own conscience regarding certain laws and practices.
   A. Discuss how this might apply to the conflicting moral issues of today.
   B. Discuss what Paul says about passing judgment on others.

5. In an age of much diversity, individuality, and different life styles, how can you, practically speaking, further the kind of patience, harmony, and being of one mind to which Paul is referring?

Challenge Questions:

1. Take any of the ideas, virtues, or exhortations which are personally meaningful in Romans, chapters 12 to 15, and share what you are called to do in ministering the Good News.

2. Compose a prayer similar to Paul's prayers in 15:6-7 and 15:13 as an expression of your faith and acceptance of the hope and peace you find in Jesus Christ.

10

Proverbs

Lesson 1 (Ch. 10, 11, and 12).

1. Identify the themes listed in question 3 with the following proverbs: 10:10; 10:17; 11:8; 11:26; 12:16; 12:20.

2. Pick out six proverbs from the reading and tell why they were meaningful to you.

3. Select from the following themes one which best fits each of the proverbs that you chose in the second question and explain your choice:
   - a. Family Virtue
   - b. Social Values
   - c. Truthfulness
   - d. Charity
   - e. Purity of Heart
   - f. Humility
   - g. Greed
   - h. Violence
   - i. Discretion of Tongue
   - j. Life and Death
   - k. Reward and Punishment

l. Wisdom
m. God and Lord
n. Work and Sloth
o. Poverty and
   Wealth
p. Patience
q. Other

Challenge Question:

4. Read 1 Corinthians 13:7, James 5:20, and 1 Peter 4:8. Compare with Proverb 10:12. What would you say is the difference in the thinking of the Old Testament wise men vs. the New Testament references?

Lesson 2 (Ch. 13, 14, and 15).

1. Select one proverb which is most relevant to you in:
   a. Your family.
   b. Your neighborhood.
   c. Your parish.
   d. The city in which you live.
   e. Society.

2. Compare Proverbs chapter 14:31 with Exodus 22:20, Leviticus 19:34, Deuteronomy 10:18, 14:28-29, and 15:7-11. What do you think the Old Testament wise men felt about the poor and being poor?

3. We find the word "fear" used in 14:26-27 and 15:33. What is your understanding of "fear of the Lord" used in this context?

4. Compare Proverbs 13:7 with Luke 12:16-21 and 12:33. What does this say about real treasure?

Challenge Question:

5. How do you think John 2:25 applies to Proverbs 15:11?

Lesson 3 (Ch. 16, 17, and 18).

1. In view of the statements made in Proverbs 16:4 and 16:7, how do you reconcile yourself with the violence and wickedness of the world today? (Refer to Rom. 9:19-23.)

2. Proverbs 16:32a: "A patient man is better than a warrior, (and he who rules his temper than he who takes a city"). List some of the ways a patient or equable Old Testament person was better than a "warrior." (See Sir. [Ecclesiasticus] 2:1-6; Job 40-41; and Pss. 16, 23, and 27.)

3. What does Proverbs 17:1 tell you about the value of a peaceful home? How is this thought extended in 17:9? Which of the ideas in the Sermon on the Mount in Matthew, chapter 5, reiterate this concept?

4. How does Proverbs 17:1 which prefers tranquility to wealth reconcile with the accepted proverbial view that riches are a reward? (See Prov. 10:2, 10:15, 16:8, 16:16, and 18:11.)

5. What lesson is there for us when Proverbs 18:23 is compared with Luke 16:19-31? What points are helpful and practical for us today?

Lesson 4 (Ch. 19, 20, and 21).

1. Proverbs 19:14 says "A home and wealth are inherited from one's forebearers, but a sensible wife is from the Lord." Do you think that the "sen-

sible wife" in the Old Testament has a positive or negative personality and position in society? Explain. (See Prov. 12:4, 18:22, 21:9, 19, 27:15-16, and 31:10-31.)

2. Israel as a nation grew out of deep poverty. Proverbs 19:17 foretells a message that is later reiterated by Matthew 25:34-40. What message does this tell the Christian about his/her personal ministry today?

3. In Proverbs 21:3, the writer speaks of the relationship of people being more important than sacrifices. See also Jeremiah 7:1-7. Using Matthew 23:23, Mark 12:33, and Romans 2:17-24, what does Jesus say about this? What does He say to you?

4. In Proverbs 20:24, man's steps are from the Lord, how then can a man understand his own ways? Humanity is dependent upon God and cannot fully foresee its own course. Express your views as to whether modern man is more or less dependent upon God than the men of the Old Testament.

5. What does Proverbs 20:10 have to say about the way we handle our daily lives relative to:
   A. Business dealings.
   B. Relations with our neighbors.

6. What does Proverbs 19:10 say about Hebrew society? Do you believe that Jesus had the same opinions as the authors of Proverbs? Explain.

Lesson 5 (22:1—24:34).

1. Proverbs 22:15 reads, "Willful ignorance is ingrained in the mind of a boy, (only) the teacher's cane will rid him of it." The English proverb, "Spare

the rod and spoil the child" is derived from this proverb and others in Proverbs. (See 13:24, 23:13-14, and 29:15.) What is the basis of the moral education for children in the Judeo-Christian tradition according to your opinion? (See Sir. [Ecclesiasticus] 30:13, Eph. 6:4.) How do you feel about this tradition in view of your experience with children's behavior?

2. 22:9, "A generous man will hear himself blessed when he gives of his own food to the needy." (See also Is. 58:6-7.) What, if anything, does the New Testament add to this proverb? (See Mat. 25:31-40 and Heb. 13:2-3.)

3. Explain what Proverbs 22:24-25 means to you. Rewrite it using the positive approach. What do you see in your own proverb that is worth emulating?

4. In 23:23, what examples can you give where truth can be bought and sold?

5. Referring to Proverbs 24:21-22 and to 1 Peter 2:17, Matthew 22:15-22, and Romans 13:1-7, when is it right not to obey authorities who are in control of government?

6. Proverbs 24:30-34 tells the story of a lazy man. Meditate and share your reflections.

Lesson 6 (25:1—27:27).

1. Many thoughts from Proverbs and other Wisdom books are seen in the New Testament as in this lesson. 25:6-7 are paralleled with Matthew 23:6-12 and Luke 14:7-11. What does this tell you about the source of Jesus' teaching?

2. After reading 25:21-22, what is your im-

mediate reaction? How do you think Paul in Romans 12:20-21 viewed this concept?

3. As 26:8 points out the dangers in giving honors to a fool, cite some instances where our society has made heroes of evil people with sad consequences.

4. Life is very complicated and we sometimes tend to rationalize what we do by saying, "God made me human. We are all sinners, but God forgives all. . . ." What are some of your ideas concerning Proverbs 26:11 and 2 Peter 2:20-22?

5. "He who digs a pit (for another) will fall into it (himself). And a stone will come back on the one who rolls it" (26:27). (See also 28:10, Eccles. 10:8-9, Pss. 7:15-17, and Sir. [Ecclesiasticus] 27:25-27.) Compare Proverbs 26:27 with the account of the adulteress (Jn. 8:1-11). Is it possible to *want* to hurt someone else without hurting yourself at the same time? Share your views.

6. What trials and suffering can you relate to Proverbs 27:8? If we consider man's home as the Old Testament sense of reaching Shalom (inner peace), what must man do to reach home?

7. It is stated in 27:23-24, "Know your flocks' condition well, take good care of your herds. . . ." Name different ways that this proverb can be applied in your family and your church today.

Lesson 7 (28:1—30:17).

1. Can you explain sin and redemption in reference to Proverbs 28:10 of the Old Testament and Romans 5:19 in the New Testament?

2. What is your understanding of 28:19?

3. What does Proverbs 29:13 tell us about God's love? (See Prov. 22:2, Mt. 5:44-45, and Jn. 4:7.)

4. A saying familiar to Americans is "In God We Trust." Proverbs 29:25-26 speaks to this idea also. What is the common wisdom here and how much does it play a part in our lives?

5. What is 30:4 trying to say? (See also Gen. 2:15-17 and Rom. 11:33.)

6. What does 30:15-16 say to you about the value of life as perceived by the Old Testament wise men? (See also Wis. 1:14-15 and 15:3.)

Lesson 8 (30:18—31:31 and 1:1—2:22).

1. Summarize the basic ideas of the following proverbs:
   A. 30:15
   B.˙ 30:18-19
   C. 30:24-28
   D. 30:29-31
Which of these categories do you identify with the most: A, B, C, or D?

2. Why does Proverbs 31:1-9 stress the avoidance of excessive drinking for rulers? (See Prov. 20:1, Sir. [Ecclesiasticus] 19:16, Is. 5:11-16, 28:7-13, and Hosea 4:11-12.) What was your reaction to the advice given in verses 6-7?

3. In view of the "freedom" some women enjoy today, how do you relate to the verses in 31:10-31, a poem in praise of the ideal wife?

4. Proverbs 31:30 says, "Charm is deceptive and beauty fleeting, the woman who fears the Lord is to be praised." What does this say to you?

5. 1:8-19 emphasizes the need to avoid bad company. How do you reconcile this with Jesus' apparent willingness to associate with "sinners"? (See Mk. 2:15-17 and Jn. 8:1-11.)

6. Wisdom speaks as a person in 1:20-33. She warns the people of Israel to reform themselves when they hear her, because when they seek her later they may not find her. Why won't they be able to find her? What connection do you see in this passage and John 7:33-34?

7. Reading 2:1-22, the Blessings of Wisdom seem to be the general theme of the passages. What relationship do you see between these passages and the practices of prayer?

Lesson 9 (3:1 — 6:19).

1. Read 3:1-6. Share your reflections on:
   A. God the Father speaking to you. How well do you heed His word?
   B. Parents talking to their children. How well do you believe children receive such messages?

2. 3:19-20 refers to the creation of the physical world. How can you reconcile God's everlasting love for us with our continued abuse of the good earth we call home?

3. As we walk with God through life our soul goes to Him weak and comes away strengthened; goes doubting and comes away satisfied; goes blind and comes away seeing. Proverbs 3:23 says, "Then you may securely go your way; your foot will never stumble." How does this apply to you?

4. Why is wisdom personified as a woman? (See 4:6-8 and 1:20-21.)

163

5. Which motives for choosing wisdom, offered in chapter 4 of Proverbs, appeal to you most? Share and explain.

6. Chapter 4 is devoted to the pursuit of wisdom; some rather terse advice is given. Can you name any specific examples in our modern life where we have condoned departure from this advice? Do you think these departures were justified in the light of present day knowledge?

7. After reading 6:1-5, can you give modern examples of events in your life which illuminate the lesson in these verses?

Lesson 10 (6:20—9:18).

1. Proverbs 6:20-30 first speaks of observing your father's command and not to forget your mother's teachings. The passage then goes into the theme of the adulterous woman and the consequences of adultery both for man and woman. Compare today's Christian/non-Christian morality with the passage.

2. In 7:3, the advice to bind the commands closely to our person was sometimes taken literally (Dt. 6:8). How do we today identify with our beliefs or commands in similar custom (e.g., wearing a cross, star of David, rings, medals)?

3. Proverbs 7 refers to the adulterous woman. Using Sirach (Ecclesiasticus) 23:22 as the Old Testament reference and John 8:1-11 as the New Testament reference, compare the two reactions. What are your reactions to the above references in view of today's relaxed morality?

4. In 8:15-21, authority requires wisdom to maintain justice for all. What virtues or qualities of wisdom do you recognize in the authority structures in your life? Explain and share.

5. Referring to 8:18-31, discuss how you see wisdom in terms of God's creation. What riches does wisdom bestow on you?

6. 8:32-36, wisdom extends "The Great Invitation."

   A. To what are we being invited?

   B. What do you believe is meant by the statement that, "All who hate me are in love with death"?

7. Do you believe wisdom is inherited or can a person acquire this quality? What does 9:1-6 say on this subject?

8. Compare wisdom in Proverbs 9:1-6 with folly in Proverbs 9:13-18.

11

Deutero-Isaiah

Lesson 1 (40:1—41:29).

1. In Matthew 3:3, the passage from Isaiah 40:3-5 is applied to the Baptizer and the Messiah, Christ. How did they "prepare" the way for the Lord? How do you? Share your reflections.

2. How would you feel bringing your everyday problems to God as He is described in Isaiah 40:12-26? How do you feel the understanding of God changed at that time and now?

3. In 40:31, what does the line "Yet those who hope upon the Lord" mean to you? What words could you use to describe your hoping in the Lord? What "new strength" have you gained in your life by placing your hope upon God? (See Mt. 11:28-29.)

4. Isaiah 41:8-16 indicates that the Lord is calling His "chosen" to Himself, that He will make their enemies as nothing, that He will avenge the suffering, slavery, persecution, and shame. In verse 10, what do the words "Uphold you with the right hand of justice" mean to you? Recognizing that the Lord has allowed His people to come to this condition, why do you think He is calling them back to Him?

5. In 41:21-25 the voices of doom cry out upon the earth. They do in our time as well as in the time of Isaiah. False prophets, worshipers of the occult, even branches of the vine feel they have discovered a different way. (Read 1 Cor. 13:2, 7-10.) What do these words and Isaiah's words on prophecy say to you?

Lesson 2 (42:1—44:23).

1. According to many scholars, a new Israel is the servant in Isaiah 42:1. List and describe the ways in which this new creation in whom God has put His Spirit (42:1 and 42:5) will bring justice to all nations as a result of His dynamic power. (Read 42:2-4 and 42:6-7.)

2. In your meditative reading of 42:10-25, what is the "new song" that needs to be sung to the Lord? What was the "old song"? Share your reflections.

3. "By paths unknown I will guide them" (42:16). Many scholars see a "new Exodus" in Isaiah 42:13-16. What "unknown paths" did the Lord reveal since then? In your estimation, what paths are still needed to be revealed? Compare the original Exodus (Ex. 12-15) to the new Exodus of Isaiah 42. How did the situation at the time of Deutero-Isaiah compare with the situation of the first Exodus. Share any Exodus experiences in your own life.

4. In 43:1-7, God promises to deliver Israel and protect her from harm. Yet, we know from history that Israel has suffered many disasters since that time. What do you think God's protection means?

Do you think this ancient promise has validity or meaning for us today?

5. 44:8 in part reads, "Is there a God besides me? There is no Rock, I know not any." How do you think the term "Rock" is used in this verse? What meaning does it have for you in your own life? (See Deut. 32:4, Is. 26:4, and Is. 17:10.)

6. How does the message concerning false idols in Isaiah 44:9-20 pertain to present days in:
   A. Industrial societies?
   B. The Church?
   C. Your parish?
   D. Your personal life?

Lesson 3 (44:24—46:13).

1. Isaiah 45:8 contains a prophetic plea that heaven and earth be enlisted and encouraged to bring forth the salvation and righteousness of the Lord. Read 42:1-4 again. How can we in our lives make justice sprout up from the soil:
   A. in our families?
   B. in our community?
   C. in the world?

2. The supreme power of God is described in 45:9-13. (Read Rom. 9:20-21 and Job 40:7-9.) Reflect on whether our questioning of God comes from our faith or out of arrogant self-assertion. Discuss the narratives of Job and Paul and how we can be more faithful.

3. In 45:18-19, we hear it said that the world was designed to be lived in and to look for the Lord among the living. What have we done with creation and how did we make it a waste land?

4. In 45:23, "To me every knee shall bend; by me every tongue shall swear," we hear that all people will be in the Kingdom of God, not just the Israelites. Assuming that you were an Israelite with the narrow view that the favor of God was for Israel alone, what would your reaction be to this idea? Can you find similar instances in our social situation today?

5. Isaiah, in verses 46:5-7, warns against false gods and idol worship. Do you think he would be irritated by anything of a similar nature in our churches and in our lives today?

6. 46:11 depicts Yahweh calling on a pagan, Cyrus the Persian, to be the instrument for salvation for His people. Share any situation in your own life in which circumstances or persons have been used by God to reveal a message or an answer to a prayer.

Lesson 4 (47:1—48:21).

1. Read 47:1-6. The Lord had allowed His people to be subjected to and enslaved by the Babylonians and now is to bring about their deliverance and punish the Babylonians. Share your thoughts on why you feel the Lord, in a manner of speaking, gave His people into their hands (47:6) and now is taunting Babylon and will take His vengeance upon them. (Read 14:4-12 known as the "Taunt Song.")

2. Chapter 47 is a lament for the ruin of Babylon. Although the prophet is referring to the ancient kingdom of Babylon, we can see Babylon as a symbol. A symbol of what? Can you call to mind other "Babylons" in history? Are there "Babylons" today?

3. In 48:1-2, the people of Israel claimed to be the people of Yahweh. Were they acting like children of God? If not, why not? What does this remind you of today?

4. Read Isaiah 48:6. What do you think are the "new and hidden things" mentioned by the Lord? Have you experienced "new and hidden things" in your life?

5. 48:17-19 shows Israel's frailty and feebleness; 48:20 and 21 demonstrates God's enduring love. (Read also Is. 54:4 and 5.) Think of examples in your own life to parallel this redeeming love of the Lord's.

Lesson 5 (49:1—50:3).

1. "Though I thought I had toiled in vain, and for nothing, uselessly spent my strength, yet my reward is with the Lord, my recompense is with my God" (Is. 49:4). What reward and/or recompense did the "servant" receive? Could you apply this passage to yourself? If so, what reward and/or recompense do you receive?

2. 49:8-13 sings a song of liberation to the captive people of Israel in Babylon. In view of what we have learned so far in Isaiah, do you feel the writer is stressing a physical liberation or a spiritual salvation?

3. 49:15 tells us that no matter what happens in our life, God will not forget us. With this in mind, why do you think we go through periods in our lives when it seems that God has abandoned us? How can Divine love apply in this situation?

4. In 49:23 we read the promise, "Those who

wait for me will not be put to shame." (See also Is. 25:9, 26:8, and 40:31, and Ps. 37:9.) Discuss in your group the ways that you can wait *for* and *on* the Lord and the results you can expect.

5. In Isaiah 50:2-3, God reasserts to Israel His infinite power. Considering the mighty signs God had already given Israel (Ex. 14:21-22, Josh. 3:16, and Ps. 105:26-45), why was it necessary for God to reaffirm His power? How does God keep reaffirming His infinite power in your life?

Lesson 6 (50:4—53:12).

1. Read 50:10-11. What message do these verses have for those who trust in self-reliance rather than in the Lord? (See Prov. 3:5-7.)

2. In 51:3-8, read that God's message is one of grace and pardon for Israel and the chance of a new beginning. In the New Testament there is added dimension to this grace and pardon by redemption. What is it? (Read Jn. 3:16.)

3. The prophet asks, "Can you forget Yahweh who is *now* making you at the same time as He is stretching out the heavens and laying the foundations of the earth" (Is. 51:13)? Do you forget? Share the reasons for your forgetfulness. How do you try to remember that you are God's people (51:16)?

4. Israel is to be relieved from the cup of wrath of God, the Babylonian captivity and exile according to 51:17-23. Why did God's chosen people have to suffer this trial?

5. In 52:2, captive Jerusalem was told to rise up and "loose the chains from around its neck." In

what ways are we captive to the things of this world? How do we go about removing the chains of this worldly captivity?

6. Isaiah 52:13—53:12 comprises one great theme of the suffering, rejected, strong and exalted servant of Yahweh. (Read also Ps. 27.) Isaiah 52:13 reads, "Behold my servant shall prosper, he shall be exalted and lifted up and shall be very high." Share in your group what the following phrases mean to you:

A. He shall be lifted up.
B. He shall be exalted.
C. And shall be very high.

What do these expressions mean in the Old Testament? (Read 1 Sam. 12:3-7 and Is. 66:2.) What did these phrases mean in relation to the New Testament? (Read Acts 22:33, Phil. 2:9, and Heb. 1:3 and 13.)

Lesson 7 (54:1—56:8).

1. In 54:6-8, God's infinite love promises to bring Israel home again, to no longer hide His face from her; rather He promises to renew her. (See Is. 40:28-31, Jer. 31:3-6, 2 Cor. 4:17, and 1 Pet. 1:6-8.) How do you view the role of suffering to the Christian life? Contrast your feelings as a Christian with those of an Israelite. How do you view renewal as the fruits of suffering in the context of these passages?

2. What is the great promise made by God to Israel in 54:14-17? Has it been fulfilled? Discuss your conclusions.

3. In 55:1-3, everyone is invited to take of food

and drink which will give life to all who partake of them and share in "an everlasting covenant." The imagery of eating and drinking to satisfy hunger and thirst is common to both the Old and New Testament. (Read Eccles. [Sirach] 24:19-21, Mt. 5:6, Ps. 42, and Jn. 7:37-38.) Comment on this imagery in the New and Old Testament? What is your feeling on hunger, then and now, and our role in making it better or worse?

4. In 55:1, read "Come and buy wine and milk without money and without price." This could be interpreted as meaning that salvation can never be bought. Meditate on this and list the ways you feel the invitation to salvation can be answered.

5. Reflect on 55:6-13, comparing it with John 1:1-18. Share your thoughts on the "word of God" in each passage.

6. 56:3-8 declaims that non-Jews (foreigners) may receive the favor of God if they serve Him. Who do you believe is being referred to in Isaiah 56:8, when God promises to gather "others" beside those already gathered to Israel?

Lesson 8 (56:9—57:21).

1. Read Isaiah 56:9-11 and John 10:1-21. Contrast and discuss the shepherds mentioned in each passage and their effects on those given into their care.

2. Discuss the contrast between the idolatry described in 57:3-13 and the idolatry of today.

3. There is a definite contrast wherein Isaiah 57:16-19 reveals God's love for His people, not as a result of merit, but of mercy and Isaiah 57:20-21

which says "no peace" for the wicked. Can you explain this? Matthew 22:14 and James 1:5-8 might give you some ideas.

Review
4. The role of the "Servant" is associated with Israel as God's chosen people. This role is clear from the following passages of Isaiah: 41:8-10, 43:3-13, 44:1-2, 44:21, and 45:4. In what way was Israel called to serve?

5. What sanctifying power of suffering can you find in the "Suffering Servant Songs"? (Read Is. 49:1-9, 50:4-11, 52:13, and 53:12.) Give your reasons for choosing these elements of suffering.

6. In 54:1-10, we read of the wonderful restoring grace of God. In verse 9 there is reference to the time of Noah when Noah and his family came forth into a new world after the deluge. (Read Gen., chapter 8.) Share in your group your thoughts on the parallel events in these two eras and any new insights you may have on God's justice and love.

Lesson 9 (58:1—60:22).

1. Israel practiced fasting as is evident from 58:3-8. What does it appear that the people expected in return for this fasting and penance? What did God require of the people? What lesson does Matthew 6:16-18 teach us about this subject? What value do you believe fasting has for us today?

2. In 58:8-11, God tells us that He desires to reveal Himself to us. In verses 8, 9, and 10 there are conditions that are to be met in order that God can reveal Himself. What does Scripture say these conditions are and how would you define them?

3. Observance of the Sabbath is discussed in Isaiah 58:13. Compare verse 13 with the New Testament references on the Sabbath, Mark 2:23-28 and Mark 3:2-6. In the light of these references, discuss how you think the Sabbath should be observed today.

4. The "Psalm of Repentance" (Is. 59:15) is a form or "examination of conscience." Take any verse and comment on it in present day terms.

5. Isaiah 59:15-16 states that the Lord is displeased that "truth is lacking" in the people and there was "no justice" and no one (man) to intervene, so the Lord prepared Himself for the judicial intervention. Read verse 17 and discuss your thoughts on how the Lord's arm brought Him victory. (See Eph. 6:13-17 and Thess. 5:8.) Explain the powers He used.

6. Read Isaiah 59:20-21 which tells of deliverance of God's earthly people and the promise of the new covenant. It is based on God's word to Abraham in Genesis 17:4. Who is the deliverer and to whom is the promise addressed? It also says that they will never cease to declare His word and bear witness for Him. Explain what is meant in these verses and how it relates in this day. (Read Jer. 31:31-34, Heb. 8:10-12 and Heb. 10:16-17.)

7. Read Isaiah 60:4-9. Note especially Isaiah 60:2b, 7b, and 9b. We read that Israel will be glorified. (Read Jn. 8:54.) What does it mean to you that God will glorify His people? Can you relate this to today? Has God glorified you as an individual? If so, how?

8. Jerusalem's new walls are to be called "Salvation" in Isaiah 60:18. What do you think salvation meant to them and what does it mean to you today?

Lesson 10 (61:1—64:11).

1. With the words in Isaiah 61:1-2, Jesus announced that the messianic era had come. (See Lk. 4:18-19.) Identifying Jesus with these verses in Isaiah, define and discuss the word "annointed" and how it pertained to Jesus.

2. Read Isaiah 61:10 and 62:5 and Luke 1:46-55. Comment on the elements making these passages come alive with joy. Make a similar prayer that will have the elements of your joy in it.

3. Read 62:10. Think about your own experiences and the obstacles and rubbish that hinder your enjoyment of free and constant access to the throne of grace and our communion with God. Share your observations.

4. Read Isaiah 63:1-10. Yahweh tells us that He alone has the power to fight evil. How can we discern and fight evil?

5. Isaiah 63:7-17 is part of a prayer.
   A. What was it telling the Israelites?
   B. Which verse in this passage has the most meaning or evokes the strongest feeling in you?

6. 64:7-8 tells us that our Father, God, is the potter and we are the clay. God desires to form each of us to His image in every aspect of our lives. Discuss the various ways God uses in molding us to His image.

Challenge Question:

In 62:2, God gives Jerusalem a new name. God does this frequently to persons in the Scriptures, e.g., Jacob-Israel, Simon-Peter, Saul-Paul. The new names usually express a new status, a new condition, a new vocation of the recipients. If God wanted to call you by another name, what would it be? Explain.

Lesson 11 (65:1—66:24).

1. In 65:1, the Lord is deliberately letting Himself be imposed upon. Share your thoughts and experiences in this area.

2. 65:13-16 continues to speak of God's reward to humble, suffering servants. Read "Beatitudes," Matthew 5:1-12, and discuss similarities that you see.

3. Read 65:25, 11:6-9, and Micah 4:3-5. How did these verses speak to the people at that time? How do they speak to us today?

4. Read 66:2 and 66:5. The passage tells us that Yahweh favors those who tremble at His word. (Also read Phil. 2:12.) What does the word "tremble" mean to you?

5. 66:7-8 compares the beginning of the new Jerusalem to the birth of a child. Why is the birth without labor?

6. 66:22 refers to the new heavens and the new earth. Other references on this are Isaiah 65:17, Hebrews 12:26-28, and Revelation 21:1. Discuss what meaning(s) these words have to you in the referenced verses.

12

Psalms

Lesson 1, Psalms: 8, 18, 102, 103, 110-118, and 148.
The Lord, His Name, Alleluia.

1. In Psalms 102 and 103 the psalmist speaks of the fatherhood of Yahweh. Seek out and share your thoughts on the passages in these psalms where you find this quality described.

2. Read Psalms 18 and 110. The psalmist uses very descriptive words to convey what God's help and victory meant to him at that time. When you are involved in a "battle" and feel the Lord's help and protection, what words do you use as a prayer of thanksgiving?

3. What do Psalms 111-113 tell you of the prayer of praising God? List some of the qualities of God you would use in praising Him in these psalms.

4. Read Psalms 115 and 116. Recall some goodness and blessing you have received from God. "How shall I make return to the Lord for all the good He has done for me" (Ps. 116:12)?

5. How do you think the descriptions of the Lord and Savior as given in Psalm 118 apply to Jesus?

6. The psalms convey something of the reverence and awe due to God. How can our prayers today express this same reverence and awe?

7. Have you ever been so touched with awe by the magnificence of the world about you that God's presence seemed so overwhelming that you felt like bursting out in praise?

Lesson 2, Psalms: 8, 33, 95, 96, 104, 139, 145, and 147.
God The Creator, His Word, His Spirit.

1. The psalmist deals with knowledge of his time in writing about creation. With our knowledge today, do you think these psalms of acclaiming God's creation lose anything? (Read Pss. 95 and 104.)

2. Read Psalm 145. Reflect on how God provides for you. How do you respond to His providence and care?

3. Comment on the many ways that the glory and power of God are expressed in Psalm 147. Share which of these speaks to you and why. What significance is there for you in verse 20?

4. Read Psalm 96. What do you think is the "new song"? How does it seem that all of creation is going to respond to this "new song"?

5. In Psalm 33 how are you encouraged to hope in the Lord?

6. Read Psalm 139. In what areas of your life are you fleeing from God? In what areas are you moving toward Him? How could this psalm become part of your daily prayer?

7. The psalmist expresses awe regarding the

high dignity of man in his likeness to God, and yet recognizes man's utter insignificance in the face of God. What, indeed, is man that God cares for him as He does?

Lesson 3, Psalms: 22, 25, 33, 37, 100, and 144.
The Lord's Plan, His People, His Promises.

1. What does Psalm 33 tell us of God's plan for His people? Are you aware of your own inheritance (v. 11-12)? Share your insights into this relationship with the Father.

2. The possessing of land and the inheritance of the earth are spoken of frequently in both the Old and New Testaments (Pss. 37:3, 11, 22, 29, and 34; Gen. 12:1, 26:3-4, 28:3-4; and Mt. 5:5). What do these promises mean to you now?

3. Read Psalm 24 meditatively. Ask yourself these questions:
   A. When I pray to my Father do I have such an intimate relationship that I acknowledge myself as the person I am, a sinner?
   B. Do I have a real sense of trust in my Father in all my requests?
   C. Is the key phrase, "your way" in my prayers?
Include these reflections in your prayer this week. Share any significant experiences.

4. Psalm 100 sings about the relationship between God and us, His people. How would you "sing" about your relationship with the Lord?

5. In Psalm 144 the psalmist asks God for pro-

tection, peace, and prosperity and in return promises praise and thanks. Do you think of yourself as especially called by God to praise Him and to carry out His plan for the salvation of mankind? Share your thoughts.

6. Frequently Psalm 22 is referred to solely as a song of lament, yet it is meant to express not only the psalmist's suffering but his relief and thanksgiving. Even when following the Father's plan for you means pain and anxiety, there is relief and opportunity for thanksgiving in the knowledge of His loving presence. Has your heart ever sung the essence of this psalm to the Lord? Share your thoughts.

Lesson 4, Psalms 77; 114, and 136. God's Redemption, Salvation, Saving Help.

1. As you read Psalm 77 recall a time in your life when you suffered a trial so intense that you actually may have felt abandoned by God like the writer of this psalm. Analyze how the psalmist reacted to this feeling. How did you react in your situation?

2. God's presence and power for His people are expressed in Psalm 114, a "Passover Song," especially by recalling some dramatic events in the history of Israel. How would you write or tell of God's presence and power through one or more dramatic events in your life history?

3. Psalm 114 recounts some of the many instances of God's power over nature recorded in the Old Testament. Share with your group one in-

stance from the Old or New Testament which particularly impresses you with God's power over nature.

4. The Psalmist remembers in Psalm 136 the common bond of salvation that the Lord worked for His people. How do we as redeemed people "give thanks to the Lord, because He is good and His love is eternal" (Ps. 136:26)?

5. "His love is everlasting" is the refrain in Psalm 136. What is your understanding of the seeming contradiction in this refrain and verses 10, 15, and 17-20?

Lesson 5, Psalms: 24, 46, 68, 85, 122, 132, and 137.
God's Presence With His People, His Glory.

One translation of Psalm 46:11 is read, "Be still, and know that I am God." Keep this verse in mind as you complete the following lesson.

1. In the beginning of Psalm 46 God is proclaimed as "our refuge and strength, an ever-present help in distress." Is He also your joy and delight, an ever-present partner in rejoicing? This week invite Him along with you in all situations. Share your experience.

2. Psalm 24 is a stirring affirmation about the relationship between God and man. Meditate especially on verses 7-10 and share your responses to receiving the king of glory.

3. Isolate a particular problem or decision in your life at this time. Pray Psalm 85 through verse

8, allowing sufficient time for silent meditation. Finish the psalm and share any insights you may have received through your prayer.

4. Read Psalm 122 meditatively. When you experience the greeting of "peace" within your Christian community, do you experience a real sense of joy and are you aware of the presence of God in each person? As suggested in verses 6-9, do you pray for his or her happiness with a real sense of community or is it just something that is required?

5. Read Psalm 137. Share how you react to being torn away from your accustomed way or setting of life. How do you affirm the Lord's fidelity even when His presence seems to be lacking?

6. In Psalm 132 the presence of Yahweh in Jerusalem parallels the presence of Christ in His Church. (Read 1 Cor. 3:16-17.) How does the awareness of the closeness of our relationship with God affect your life?

Lesson 6, Psalms: 1, 19, 26, 111, and 119.
Covenant, Sacrifice, Law.

1. What does "the fear of God is the beginning of wisdom" mean to you (Ps. 111:10 and Prov. 1:7)?

2. The happy abider in God's law is "like a tree planted by water streams, yielding its fruit in season" (Ps. 1:3). In relating the "water streams" to baptism, what fruits are yielded in season? What values does Psalm 1 emphasize for commitment to the Lord?

3. How does the psalmist express his loyalty and

devotion to God in Psalm 26? This is not a proud expression of his worthiness but a true acknowledgment of God's gift of faithfulness. How could you acknowledge God's faithfulness to you today?

4. The marvel of the law of the Lord refreshes the soul (Ps. 19:8). Examine your outlook on the law of the Lord as described in Psalm 19. Is your soul refreshed with this marvel? How can we become generally more appreciative and grateful for God's law as the psalmist is in Psalm 19?

5. Sometimes we feel bound by rules and regulations. How is the psalmist's understanding of the law one of love and hunger for God rather than of legalism? How can we find the life and freedom suggested in Psalm 119:93 and John 8:31-32 and still live according to God's law? How does Jesus help us fulfill the law (Mt. 5:17)?

6. Read through Psalm 119. The psalmist seeks through repetition of the ideas and aspirations to raise one's soul to loving contemplations of God's goodness. Why do you think it might be a starting point for personal prayer? Share your feelings about this style of prayer.

Lesson 7, Psalms: 32, 51, 81, 94, 103, and 130.
The Lord's Merciful Love.

1. After confessing our sins and experiencing God's forgiveness and joyous freedom, what does the psalmist ask us to do and what encouragement does he give us in Psalm 32?

2. A person's longing to be released from sin is expressed several times in Psalm 51. What does the

Lord require of you that you may be one with Him? How do you ask for God's forgiveness?

3. Psalm 81 was composed for the feast of the Tabernacles, one of ancient Israel's most important holidays. How does this psalm contrast the joy the Israelites found in worshiping the Lord with the solemn responsibility they had as His chosen people? How is God's love for His people brought out in this psalm?

4. God's love and mercy are often shown by His seeing and listening to our plight (Ps. 94:8-9, Mt. 13:14-17, and Is. 6:9-10). What does compassionate seeing and listening mean in your life?

5. God's love is superior to natural human love, yet we are called to love and follow His example (Jn. 17:25-26). As you read Psalm 103, for which example do you feel you need the most help from the Lord in passing love on to others?

6. Read Psalm 130. How can we share the mercy and love with those who do not believe, hope in, or love God?

Lesson 8, Psalms: 6, 10, 13, 30, 38, 39, 44, 64, 73, and 88.
The Mystery of Suffering in Human Life.

1. Sickness, affliction, and injustice were seen in the Old Testament as the effects and punishment of sin.
   A. Discuss how this is portrayed in Psalms 13, 38, 39, and 44.
   B. How do you as a Christian approach this dilemma?

2. It is a mystery how the wicked prosper in a world that God loves. Yet it is just as much a mystery how those who are oppressed by the wicked still praise the Lord. Read Psalms 10 and 64 and contemplate these contradictions.

3. Have you ever almost lost your balance (Ps. 73:2)? How did God show His goodness to you in setting you aright? How can you help someone else in a similar crisis?

4. Compare the expressions of endless afflictions in Psalm 88 and Job 30. How were you affected by this reading? What testimony of deep personal faith and humble trust can you find even in this type of approach to God amidst so much affliction? Does this relate in any way to your life of faith today?

5. Sometimes when we feel secure or complacent (Ps. 30:7) God calls us to suffering. As you read this psalm, recall some trial or suffering in your lifetime. How did that experience call you to grow?

6. Psalm 6, one of the seven penitential psalms, is an individual lament. Its structure contains four elements:

    A. A complaint and cry for help.
    B. A plea to the Lord and a reason why He should help.
    C. A more detailed description to move the Lord.
    D. The Lord has heard the prayer.

Compose a simple lament of your own following this structure. What meaning does "your" psalm have for you?

Lesson 9, Psalms: 2, 21, 24, 45, 72, and 110.
The Messiah.

1. The universal reign of the Messiah is decreed in Psalm 2. Does the universe of your being feel the power of His rule? Do you have nations (within or without) which conspire together against the Lord; and those which rejoice and take refuge?

2. Psalms 21 and 110 speak strongly of an earthly kingdom where all the enemies are shattered and destroyed. Yet there are elements in these psalms which indicate that Christ's kingdom is more than just the destruction of His enemies. What are some of these deeper elements accompanying the coming of His kingdom?

3. "The Kingdom of God is at hand" (Mt. 3:3). If we give this statement real meaning even today, what aspects of His kingdom in Psalm 72 do you cherish or long for in your life or the lives of others? What responsibility do you have for establishing this kingdom?

4. Psalm 45 is a love song for the king's wedding day. After reading this psalm slowly, share with the group how you think it glorifies God.

5. What qualities and experiences of your relationship with Jesus are called forth in Psalm 24? What feelings of celebration are awakened in you as you simply pray this psalm?

6. In the psalms of this lesson the Messiah is described and foretold as *the* annointed one, *the* teacher, and *the* leader. How do you see Jesus in His

life fulfilling these roles? How do you see His ministers of today carrying on this mission?

Lesson 10, Psalms: 16, 22, 31, 40, 69, 116, and 188.
The Servant of The Lord.

1. Both Psalm 31 and Psalm 69 relate to the anguish of Jesus, "the suffering servant."
   A. How do these psalms help you find comfort in your suffering?
   B. How does an awareness of Jesus' suffering help you?
   C. How do you help others in their suffering?
2. Hebrews 10:5-9 uses Psalm 40:7-9 to describe the essence of Jesus' ministry, which is that to do God's will is His delight and joy. How does this joy and delight exist in your life as you see God's will fulfilled?
3. In your deepest distress and sorrow, have you ever cried "O Lord, save my life!" (Ps. 116:4) and then felt the Lord's calming hand upon your spirit? Share your experience.
4. We rejoice the Christ, the rejected stone, is now the cornerstone of our faith (Ps. 118:22-23). Reflect upon the human Jesus and the incidents of rejection He experienced.
   A. How do you imagine He felt?
   B. What sustained Him through these times?
   C. What are your reactions to personal rejection?
   D. What sustains you?
5. Psalm 22 is one of the better known psalms concerning the "suffering servant." It encompasses

the heights and the depths of the meaning of servant. What does being a servant mean to you?

6. In the preceding questions we have dealt with the theme of "servant," especially the suffering servant. The relationship between God and man is more than that of master and servant. A family relationship is nearly inferred in Psalm 16:6. Reflect upon this and upon John 15:15-17. What does this dimension of servanthood mean to you?

Lesson 11, Psalms: 65, 67, 87, 96, 97, and 98.
The Church, The Salvation of The Nations, The Coming of The Kingdom.

1. Which symbols in Psalm 65 do you think refer to the Church, the salvation of the nations, and the coming of the kingdom?

2. In the psalms the terms nations and peoples often refer to all peoples, not just the people of Israel. What does Psalm 67 have to say about the extent and character of God's kingdom? Compare this psalm with the Lord's Prayer (Mt. 6:9-13).

3. A joyful union of people and nations is the cause for song in Psalm 87. Has that sense of oneness with all people ever overtaken you? Share the experience and understanding you have about this.

4. Psalm 96 is a happy proclamation of God's wonders. How does your community of believers proclaim and praise God's goodness? What part do you play in this proclamation?

5. Both Psalm 97 and Psalm 98 speak of the victory of the Lord. His salvation and history seem closely bound to the qualities of justice, kindness,

and equality. Do you see much evidence of this victory in the world today? How do you struggle with these qualities in your own life in order that this victory may begin now?

6. Psalm 98 calls on the whole earth, even inanimate creation to sing and rejoice over God's faithfulness, mercy, and truth. Share what personal joy this gives you.

Lesson 12, Psalms: 25, 27, 91, 100, 116, and 117.
The Lord's Faithfulness to His Promises.

1. Psalms 100 and 117 are calls to praise God for His kindness and faithfulness. Think about all the facets of faithfulness which have meaning for you. With whom do you have a faithful relationship?

2. Psalm 100:3 says, "Know that the Lord is God." What promises do you think are implied in this phrase?

3. Trust and patience in the Lord are indicated as dispositions of the psalmist in Psalm 25. How do you experience and struggle with the "waiting on the Lord" in your own life? For what are you waiting? What have you learned by waiting?

4. Psalm 27 is an expression of trust in God's integrity to extend His power of protection over His people. Does this psalm strike you as sad or cheerful? Which verse in this psalm is most meaningful to you?

5. Meditate on Psalm 116. How can you respond to the direction of verse 7? Why do you think the psalmist is asking you to do this?

6. Read Psalm 91:1-13 as a prayer reflecting the benefits of one who trusts in God. Read verses 14-16 as God answering you. Share your thoughts.

Challenge Question:

Read Hebrews 10:35—12:2 about Old Testament figures responding in faith to God's promises. Put into today's terms how you view faith and how you respond in faith to God's call and promise.

Lesson 13, Psalms: 29, 34, 36, 63, 84, 103, and 111.
In Fear And Praise Of The Lord.

1. Read Psalm 29. How do you respond to this God who speaks from a vantage point of majesty and power, with a voice thundering and mighty? In what way have you experienced this aspect of God's power (thundering) in your life? How do you respond to a more gentle approach of God?

2. "Come, children, hear me; I will teach you the fear of the Lord" (Ps. 34:12). What does this psalm teach:

    A. About fear and praise of the Lord?

    B. About God's relationship with His people?

3. Read Psalms 63 and 84.

    A. How do you identify with the strong and fervent desires of the psalmists? Reflect on your life as that of a pilgrim yearning for the joy of beholding the face of God.

    B. Have you ever been in the psalmist's position, far away from the temple and homesick for the shelter of His sanctuary and the refuge of His altar? What is there within us or in our life experience that sometimes creates this nostalgic longing for God's intimacy?

4. Psalm 111 is a hymn of praise. Verse 10 states that fear of God is the beginning of wisdom. What is your understanding of this? How do you think you could be led to praise God through fear of Him?

5. Read Psalm 103. What more can you say about the AWESOMENESS of God? Try.

Lesson 14, The Songs of The New Testament.
The Benedictus—Luke 1:68-79, The Magnificat—Luke 1:46-55, The Nunc Dimittis—Luke 2:29-32.

1. Read the Canticle of Zechariah, the Benedictus in Luke 1:68-79. When your fundamental, longed-for hopes are reaching fulfillment, how would you praise the Lord in thanksgiving? For what specifically would you be praising God?

2. Look at the titles of all the past lessons on psalms and think about the meaning of each title. Now read Luke 1:67-80 and share what meaning the psalms have given you to help you to a fuller understanding of Zechariah's Canticle.

3. Compare the Magnificat (Lk. 1:46-55) with the Canticle of Hannah in 1 Samuel 2:1-10. How are they so similar yet so different?

4. In the Magnificat, Mary, with deep humility, praises God's mercy, power, and fidelity. Share what meaning these qualities of God have for you.

5. In response to God's call and special gifts to you write your own Magnificat beginning with the

words, "My being proclaims the greatness of the Lord. . . ."

6. The passage in Luke known as the "Nunc Dimittis" (Lk. 2:29-32) is followed by the prophecy of Simeon (Lk. 2:33-35). What do you believe caused Simeon to say these things about Jesus to His parents? What effect do you think it had on them?

7. Three themes are present in Simeon's song:
A. God's faithfulness to His promises.
B. God's act of salvation.
C. The universality of salvation.

How are these themes reflected in Jesus' ministry? How are they reflected in the Church ministry? How do you see them reflected in your own life?

Lesson 15, Psalms: 23, 25, 27, 33, 34, 42, 47, 84, 85, 95, 96, 97, and 98. The Psalms and the Liturgy.

1. Psalm 23 implies the Lord's loving and pastoral care that is given to us through His Church. As you read this psalm, what sacramental and eucharistic images or symbols come to your mind that are an important part of the Church's care for you?

2. Psalms 25 and 27 are used often throughout the year in worship or liturgy. Identify the themes present in these psalms and comment on what makes them versatile and meaningful.

3. Psalm 33 has an intricate structure: A summons to praise (vs. 1-3), the theme of the word of the Lord (vs. 4-9), the theme of the plan of the Lord (vs. 10-12), the sight of the Lord (vs. 13-19), and a hymn to hope (vs. 20-22). Why would these themes

be so valuable and relevant as part of a church service or liturgy?

4. Psalms 42 and 43 were originally a single psalm expressing a deep longing to be out of exile and within the temple to praise God. When have you felt such a need to share your praises with others? In the light of this need for community worship, why do you think these psalms would often be chosen to begin a liturgy?

5. The favor of God is the foundation and source of all of our happiness. As you reflect on Psalms 84 and 85, share what makes you happy and fulfilled in God. How could this happiness be expressed in a community celebration?

6. Psalms 95, 96, 97, and 98 are all strong calls to join in community praise and worship. What do you feel the community as a whole is called to? What do you feel is your personal response to the Father in these psalms?

N.B. This unit on the psalms was developed from the format (titles) of "Key to the Psalms" by M. Perkins Ryan so the lessons follow the titles of her chapter. However since her references to the psalms are in the old style numeration, we have listed psalms on the lesson sheets according to the more modern numeration. Other useful bibliographical items:

  1957—Ryan, M.P. Key to the Psalms, Liturgical Press, Collegeville, Minn.
  1968—Ellison, H.L. The Psalms, Wm. Eerdmans Pul., Grand Rapids, Mich.
  1967—MacKenzie, R.A.F. The Book of the Psalms, (O.T. Reading Guide,) Liturgical Press, Collegeville, Minn.

Appendices

Appendix 1

1. Orientation for New Members

Purposes of the orientation session:
  A. To acquaint *new/prospective* participants who come after the program has officially begun, with the S.O.S. program and what it offers.
  B. To put them at ease regarding what is expected in terms of personal performance, personal challenges, and
  C. To allow an opportunity for expressing concerns and questions.

Considerations:
  A. This outline is specific to the program at Mount Mary Immaculate. It has evolved partly out of my own enthusiasms/prejudices, and does not include a special question/answer period. Because the groups are small, I use a discussion format wherein questions from the group are appropriate at any time. This is helpful in assessing the group and adjusting the presentation as necessary—known as "playing it by ear"—therefore . . .
  B. The presentation varies considerably, according to the interests, needs, and previ-

ous experience with Scripture of each morning's participants within the following (general) outline.

2. Individual Introductions

A. Who are you?
B. Why did you come?
C. What do you expect?

3. The Program

A. An ongoing event.
B. Information about the book being studied currently.
C. The schedule—times and places.

The Small Group Discussion

A. Purpose and benefits.
B. Material discussed—based on "lesson."
C. Personal perceptions.
D. Learning from others.

The Lecture

An academic pursuit, not intended to answer the "lesson" questions; information about the speaker.

The Mass

A. Using same Scripture studied in discussion group and lecture.
B. The unique character of the S.O.S. which affords an opportunity to examine a part of Scripture in the three ways above and as follows:

4. Uses of Scripture

Explanation of mimeographed sheet distributed to all newcomers.

Contemplative use, exemplified by the discussion group.
- A. God speaks to us personally through His Holy Word.
- B. The Holy Spirit makes Jesus' message continually relevant for each generation.

(Because the groups of newcomers to the Mount have regularly included Christians who are not Catholic or who are converts to Catholicism, I have found it helpful to discuss the Protestant tradition of referring to Scripture for personal guidance and instruction and the Catholic tradition of reliance on the Church for interpretation of Scripture. There seems to be much willingness to share experiences [and concerns] in this area.)

Exegetical use, exemplified by the lecture. Academic approach to Scripture, a study including . . .

- A. Understanding the author, the audience, their times, culture, beliefs, and attitudes.
- B. Analysis of literary style, technique, and mechanisms.
- C. Purpose of the writings, the author's intent and meaning.

Liturgical use, Scripture in the formal worship of the Church.

5. Elaboration on the discussion groups

Discussion of fears/apprehensions commonly encountered.

    A. Risking exposing oneself.

    B. Risking change.

    C. Coming into an established group.

    D. Sharing in the group.

    E. Freedom from censure.

    F. Value of the individual and appreciating differences (see level).

    G. Freedom from obligation to share vs. concept of letting God work through us by offering ourselves to others in love.

    H. "Homework" or the "lesson" as a tool for precipitating contemplative use of assigned text emphasis on freedom from right and wrong answers.

6. Scripture Itself

Brief overview (only occasionally indicated).

    A. Old Testament, a collection of books (history, poetry, prophecy, legend, and law) about the agreement between God (Yahweh) and man (the Hebrews) written in different places over some 900 years to teach religious truths, patriotism, describe the Messiah, etc.

B. New Testament, stories and teachings about a new agreement between God and people based on the teachings and life of Jesus.
C. Gospels—the Good News written for believers.
D. Acts—History of the early Church.
E. Letters—to churches, individuals.
F. Revelation—a "vision."

7. Mechanics of Scripture (recommended).

A. Variations in translations (may be encountered in discussion group).
B. Emergence of paraphrase.
C. Books omitted.
D. Variations in titles of books.
E. Exercise in finding passages—book, chapter, verse.

compiled by Chris Horner

Appendix 2

Samples of Mini Bible Study Column

The Greek Fathers of the Church considered the formation of the Christian person to stem from the unceasing study of the Bible. "Sharing of Scripture," a modern successful Scripture-study program in the Oakland diocese, feels the same way. Started in 1973, we now want to expand that sharing concept to the readers of CATHOLIC CHARISMATIC for use in mini-group Bible study.

The word "sharing" implies that whatever insights and gifts the Lord has given us must in turn be given to others, so we pass them on, perhaps for home study with family or with friends.

Recommended Format:

1. During the week, each person should answer the questions prayerfully and individually.

2. At the weekly meeting, share your answers with members of your group. (Encourage new members to join your group at any point in the series.)

3. After doing (1) and (2) as a mini-group, appoint a member to read the commentaries below:

A. *The Acts of the Apostles* by Neal M. Flanagan, O.S.M. (NF), The Liturgical Press.

B. *The Acts of the Apostles* (revised 1976) by William Barclay (WB) The Westminster Press.

C. *Dictionary of the Bible* by John L. McKenzie, S.J. (MJc), Macmillan Publishing Co., Inc.

4. Discuss any difficulties or new insights.

1st Week: Read Acts 1:1-11 How did the apostles misunderstand the "Kingdom of God" in Acts 1:6? (See also Lk. 17:20-21.) Do you find yourself in the same position as the apostles in Acts 1:18-11? How or why not? *Resource Material/Indicators:* The book of Acts is not concerned with giving us a fact-filled history. Rather, it tries to capture the spirit, the problems, and the expansion of the early Church. Luke is correcting the commonly-held notion that Jesus would shortly return. He describes an era of witness under the guidance of the Spirit—the time of the Church. What Acts wants to do is give us a "series of typical exploits and adventures of the great heroic figures of the early Church." (Cf. Wm. Barclay, THE ACTS OF THE APOSTLES: The Westminster Press, 1955, p. xiii.) Read and discuss NF & WB 1:1-11.

2nd Week: Read Acts 1:12-2:47. Acts 2:1-13 describes Pentecost. What does Pentecost mean to you? Compare early Christian community with today's Christian community (Acts 2:42-47). *Resource Material/Indicators:* All those who were close to Jesus and those later converted were an integral part of the community and received the Spirit on Pentecost. The Spirit working through men brings about the new age of Church and mission: the message lived and proclaimed. (See NF 2:5-13.) Note that the early Christians had not left the Jewish religion (see NF 2:42-47). Read and discuss NF & WB 1:12-2:47.

3rd Week: Read Acts 3:1-4:31. What problems do you face in your community (Acts 4:1-12)? What are some ways we as Christians can proclaim this message in addition to using words (Acts 4:29)? *Resource Material/Indicators:* The emphasis of miracle stories is not on the physical healing but on the healing power of Jesus Christ as a means of awakening faith. The use of the Old Testament references shows that God's plan of reconciliation is coming to completion and that the God who acted in the Jews' history has acted in the life of Jesus and acts in the lives of the apostles. (See NF 3:1-26.) Conversion is a turning away *from* self-centeredness and a turning *to* the Father. (See JMc "Pharisees," "Scribe," & "Sadducees.") Read and discuss NF & WB 3:1-4:31.

4th Week: Read Acts 4:32-5:42. How do honesty, trust, and responsibility fit into your community commitment (Acts 5:1-11)? Why do you suppose the Sanhedrin felt they must do something about these people (Acts: 4:15—5:35)? *Resource Material/Indicators:* Community life and not being possessed by the material world are central in living the Jesus message. The Spirit lives in the community and compels one to face one's good points and faults: The Christians were just one Jewish sect among several which existed in Jerusalem before 70 A.D. Read and discuss NF & WB 4:32-5:16.

5th Week: Read Acts 6:1-8:3. What does Acts 6:1 tell us about the early Christian community that hasn't been told before? What do you see to be the religious significance of chapters 6 and 7? *Resource Material/Indicators:* The structure of the Christian community is mainly the result of cultural influence and responds to the various needs of the people. Stephen's martyrdom is the final crisis which results in Christianity's separation from Judaism and forces the apostles to preach outside of Jerusalem (ref. NF 7:59-60). Read and discuss NF & WB 6:1-8:3.

6th Week: Read Acts 8:4-9:19. How do you react to Simon's attempt (Acts 8:14-21) to buy the power of the Spirit? The Lord chose to convert Paul himself, and not through His disciples (Acts 9:1-19). What could we learn from this? *Resource Material/Indicators:* The conversion of these Jewish outcasts (the eunuch and Samaritans) is contrasted with the "chosen People of God's" (Israel) rejection. Paul's receiving and acceptance of the Spirit make him a part of the Christian community. The Spirit is a free gift from the Father. Read and discuss NF & WB 8:4-9:19.

7th Week: Read Acts 9:20-43. Why do you think the disciples behaved as they did in Acts 9:26? (See Mt. 18:21-22.) Why do you think the first century Church experienced so many miracles? *Resource Material/Indicators:* The miracles performed by Peter are reminiscent of those performed by Jesus and tell the reader that Jesus continues to act through Peter. In the New Testament the term "saints" does not refer to people who have attained heaven but to ordinary people who have turned to Jesus in faith (Christians). Read and discuss NF & WB 9:20-43.

8th Week: Read Acts 10:1-11:18. How do you react to persons whose opinions you do not value receiving the grace of the Holy Spirit? What religious significance or value do you find in chapter 10? *Resource Material/Indicators:* In Luke's theology, Peter, an eyewitness to the life of Jesus and leader of the Jerusalem community, must inaugurate the mission to the Gentiles for it to be valid. The conferring of the Spirit by God on Cornelius and his household signifies that God has put his seal of approval on the mission to the Gentiles. To associate with non-Jews was a stumbling block for Peter and all devout Jews because non-Jews were not considered part of God's elect. In Jesus all these distinctions are abolished. Read and discuss: NF & WB 10:1-11:18.

Recommended Format:

1. During the week, each person should answer the questions prayerfully and individually.

2. At the weekly meeting, share your answers with members of your group. (Encourage new members to join your group at any point in the series.)

After doing (1) and (2) as a mini-group, appoint a member to read the commentaries listed below:

    A. *The Acts of the Apostles* by Neal M. Flanagan, O.S.M. (NF), The Liturgical Press.

B. *The Acts of the Apostles* (revised 1976) by William Barclay (WB), The Westminster Press.
C. *Dictionary of the Bible* by John L. McKenzie, S.J. (JMc), Macmillan Publishing Co., Inc.
4. Discuss any difficulties or new insights.

9th WEEK: READ ACTS 11:19—13:12. (Acts 11:19-30) How does the message proclaimed to the Greeks differ from Peter's message to the Jews (Acts 2:14-41)? What does Peter's imprisonment story tell us about our own imprisonment or lack of freedom (Acts 12:5-17; also see Jn. 8:32)?

Resource Material/Indicators: Originally all preaching and missionary activity stemmed from and was performed under the approval of the Jerusalem community. Gradually the community at Antioch gained prominence, becoming the home base for the mission to the Gentiles. It is at Antioch that the followers of Jesus are first called Christians, which indicates that they are assuming an identity separate from Judaism and a worship separate from the Temple. (See NF 11:25-26.) The imagery used in portraying Herod's (Agrippa I) (see NF 12:20-24) death was a common literary style used to convey the awful death of those who boldly stood against God. Read/Discuss: NF and WB 11:19—13:12.

10th WEEK: READ ACTS 13:13—14:28. (A) Read Acts 13:16-25; then reflect on your own history of encounters with God. (B) Share your idea of God as Father. What does it mean to you? (See Ps. 2:7, Acts 13:33-34, JMc "Father," II, p. 275.) In

Acts 14:8-18, adoration quickly turns to hatred.
What do you make of it?

Resource Material/Indicators: Paul's speech reflects the speeches of Peter (2:14-36) and Stephen
(7:1-53) (see NF "f " p. 5). The promises that were
made to the Jews have been fulfilled in Jesus' life
and ministry. Through His death and resurrection
God offers His life-giving love to those who believe.
Rejection and persecution did not discourage Paul
or repress God's Word but spurred him on to other
regions and peoples. The tearing of one's garments
is a Jewish sign of displeasure, and the term "living God" (Acts 14:15) is a Jewish expression dis-
tinguishing the "true God" from false gods.
Read/Discuss: NF and WB 13:13—14:28.

11th WEEK: READ ACTS 15:1—16:5. What was
the point of the controversy in Acts 15:1-5? What
was the solution given in Acts 15:28-29? Why do
you think practices such as circumcision and
dietary observances could be such a source of turmoil? Do we see this conflict in our own parish
communities?

Resource Material/Indicators: Paul, leader of
the Gentile mission, now becomes the main character of Acts while the Jerusalem community and
its leaders fade into the background. (See JMc
"Paul" and NF "St. Paul's Life," pp. 9-11 and "St.
Paul's Epistles," pp.18-21.) It should be remembered
that the Holy Spirit is the central character of Acts
(see NF "D" p. 15). Paul's account of the apostolic
council (see Gal. 1:19—2:10) differs in facts, tone,

and outcome, for he knows nothing of the provisions proposed by James. The rejection of the necessity of circumcision means that one becomes righteous through faith and not by adherence to laws. After the council, James, the brother of the Lord, becomes the head of the Jerusalem community. Read/Discuss: NF and WB 15:1—16:5.

12TH WEEK: READ ACTS 16:6—17:9. What is the point of the story of Paul's imprisonment in Philippi (Acts 16:16-24)? Why do you suppose Paul insisted upon his rights as a Roman citizen (Acts 16:35-39)? Share any situation in your life that may relate to this.

Resource Material/Indicators: The possibility of Luke being a companion of Paul is often criticized because Luke's accounts of Paul's journeys and basic concepts differ from Paul's own accounts in his letters. An interesting note is the mention of the women converts which indicates a practical application of there not being any distinction between sexes in the salvation of Jesus Christ (see Gal. 3:28). Also, women bringing others to faith in Jesus Christ was as noteworthy as when men did it. Read/Discuss: NB and WB 16:6—17:9.

13TH WEEK: READ ACTS 17:10—18:23. Why do you think Paul was unsuccessful with the men of Athens (Acts 17:22-32)? In Acts 18:22-23 Paul finishes his second journey and begins his third. What do you feel are Paul's most important accomplishments thus far and why?

Resource Material/Indicators: For Luke, the Good News had to be first preached to the Jews. Eventually, Christianity developed views which could no longer be assimilated into Judaism (e.g., positions on Jesus as Messiah and the law). This resulted in a break with Judaism and an emphasis on Christianity's universalistic nature and the Gentile mission. Athens, representing the Greek religion and thought, is the location for this example of the opposition Christianity met from Greek philosophy (see JMc "Greek" and 1 Cor. 1:18-25). Because the Greeks were not familiar with the Old Testament, Paul used both Greek philosophy and Old Testament terms in his preaching, thus developing a new wording which was understandable to the Gentiles (cf. Acts 13:17-41 with 1 Cor. 8:6) Read/Discuss: NF and WB 17:10—18:23.

14TH WEEK: READ ACTS 18:24—19:20. What is the significance of the laying of hands on the newly committed Christian (Acts 19:6; also see Acts 2:4; 8:15-17; 11:27; 1 Tim. 4:14 and NB 27:18-23)? What message do you receive from the verses in Acts 19:13-20?

Resource Material/Indicator-: Miracles are signs of the power of Jesus, which is the power of God, present in the individual or community. Faith in Jesus Christ, freeing us from the limits of our humanity and from our restrictive life-styles, allows us to grow because we are open to both God and others. (See JMc "Miracles."). Ephesus was known for its spells and magical arts (see WB 18:24-28 "In Ephesus"). In the New Testament, exorcism in the name of Jesus Christ signifies that God's reign is present, and, because of this, evil is losing its power over all creation (see WB 19:13-20). Read/Discuss: NF and WB 18:24—19:20.

15TH WEEK: READ ACTS 19:21—21:14 What feelings in your life can you relate to the incident of Paul's parting with his beloved disciples who did not expect to see him again (Acts 20:25-38)? In Acts 21:4-6, why was Paul determined to go to Jerusalem, knowing the fate that awaited him (Acts 21:11-14; also see Mt. 16:21-23)?

Resource Material/Indicators: Because Jerusalem was central in Judaism, Luke emphasizes it as the birthplace of Christianity, thus showing that the time of the Church follows from the time of Israel. (See JMc "Jerusalem"—*6. Jerusalem as a Theological Symbol.*) The Christian community, a people concretely bound together through faith and God's love, believed that all aspects of creation should be enjoyed and shared, but should never become so central to one's life that they could not be given up or left behind (see WB 19:21-22). Paul's speech in Ephesus indicates what leaders of the Christian community in all ages should be—guides and servants of the people, not powerful lords and rulers. Elders, respected men with a sound understanding of life, were chosen to guide the community. Read/Discuss: NF and WB 19:21—21:14.

16TH WEEK: READ ACTS 21:15—23:11. Why were the Jewish Christians, especially in Jerusalem, so reluctant to leave the old law (Acts 21:20-25; also see Pss. 19:7-11 and Acts 15:10-11)? Compare the accounts of Paul's conversion stories in Acts 9:1-30. 22:3-16, and 26:12-18. What do you make of the differences?

Resource Material/Indicators: Many Christians no longer viewed the Law, which was the Jewish source of all human and divine knowledge, as the mediator of salvation, but considered Jesus to be this. (See JMc "Law"—7. *Torah in Judaism* and 8. *Law in NT*.) A problem arose because many Jewish-Christians believed that the Law still must be followed. (See NF 21:17.) The Sanhedrin was the major Jewish council which ruled on both religious and secular issues. (See JMc "Council".) Read/Discuss: NF and WB 21:15—23:11.

Recommended Format

1. During the week prior to your meeting, each person should answer the questions prayerfully and individually.

2. At the weekly meeting, share your answers with the members of your group. Encourage new members to join your group at any point in the series.

3. Have the previously appointed member [see (5) below] read aloud the "Resource Material/ Indicators" and share whatever insights he or she received from the material "For Further Study."

4. Discuss any difficulties or new insights.

5. Appoint a group member to read before your next meeting the material indicated "For Further Study" and to share insights with your group after the general sharing. This position may be rotated. Your group will need the following books "For Further Study":

A. (JMc) *Dictionary of the Bible* by John L. McKenzie, S.J., Macmillan Publishing Co.

B. (NF) *The Acts of the Apostles* by Neal M. Flanagan, O.S.M., The Liturgical Press.

C. (WB) *The Acts of the Apostles* (Revised 1976) and *The Letters to the Galatians and Ephesians* (Revised 1976) by William Barclay, The Westminster Press.

D. (AC) *The Epistle of Paul to the Galatians* by Alan Cole, Wm. B. Eerdmans Publishing Company.

17TH WEEK: READ ACTS 23:12—26:32. How, when, and where do you find yourself most open to God's will? By the end of chapter 26, how do you think Paul views the relationship between Judaism and Christianity?

Resource Material/Indicators: Luke shows Christianity as Judaism's fulfillment by portraying the resurrection of the dead as being central to both Christianity and Pharasaic Judaism (see NF 24:10-16). Thus the Jews' case against Paul seems ironical because he is being tried for preaching about the very thing they (Jews) have been awaiting. Felix was breaking the law by continuing to hold Paul because one could only be held two years

213

without a sentence. Being a Roman citizen, a change in venue could not be forced upon Paul; he also had the option of having his case heard by the Roman imperial tribunal. Paul's court scenes reflect the conditions for Jesus' followers mentioned in Luke 21:12. *For Further Study:* See JMc, "ROME." Read NF and WB 23:12—26:32.

18TH WEEK: READ ACTS 27:1—28:31. Why does Paul go to the Jews first in Rome in Acts 28:17? Now that you are completing your study of Acts, how well do you think the apostles fulfilled the mission with which the Lord entrusted them in Acts 1:8?

Resource Material/Indicators: Paul's decision to go to Rome, the capital of the known world, fulfills the command in Acts 1:8 to preach the Good News to the "ends of the earth." Luke uses the safety offered to those who travel with Paul to Rome (Acts 27:21-26) to imply to his readers that salvation is offered to all men who accompany Paul. Reconciliation with God is given not just to the Jews but to any person who listens and accepts. In Rome Paul is given the opportunity for the last time to challenge the Jews and to defend himself in their presence. Luke's history of Jesus (Gospel) and the early Church (Acts) shows how he was able to allow the word of God in Jesus to aid and challenge the Christian community of his day. Also, it indicates that the early Christians no longer saw themselves as an insignificant sect, but as a people with a religion that was for the people of all nations. *For Further Study:* See Jmc, "ACTS OF THE APOS-

TLES"—introductory paragraph, Read NF and WB 27:1—28:31.

1ST WEEK: READ GALATIANS 1:1—1:24. Compare Paul's conversion account (Gal. 1:11-24) with Luke's account in Acts 9:1-19 and 22:6-16. What do you suppose was happening in the churches in Galatia to arouse such indignation in Paul?

Resource Material/Indicators: Paul is probably writing to the people of the northern section of the province of Galatia in Asia Minor. In this letter (written around 54 A.D.) Paul first rebuffs the Galatians for allowing themselves to fall prey to the Judaizers and then tenaciously rebukes this group's claims, which include: (a) that Christians must be circumcised in order to be reconciled to God, (b) that certain Jewish holy days must be observed, and (c) that angels must be venerated. The Judaizers also falsely claimed that Paul, since he did not know Jesus during His ministry and was not present at His resurrection and ascension, is not an apostle and cannot claim the authority of one. Paul recounts his conversion experience and subsequent trip to Jerusalem because he is very adamant about the *fact* that he was personally commissioned by the risen Jesus and that he does not have to rely upon the "Twelve" or any other human source for either the content or authority of his message. *For Further Study:* See JMc, "GALATIA" and "GALATIANS"; WB Introduction, "THE JUDAIZERS." Read WB and AC 1:1—1:24.

2ND WEEK: READ GALATIANS 2:1—2:21. Contrast the characters of Peter and Paul as seen in chapter 2. Why do you suppose that Paul felt it imperative to correct Peter's behavior in Galatians 2:11-14?

Resource Material/Indicators: The Jerusalem council was held to quell the conflict within the early Christian communities on whether the non-Jews entering the Christian faith must be circumcised—i.e., become a Jew in order to become a Christian. Paul's account of this discussion differs from Luke's account in Acts 15:1-26. Peter, a "pillar" of the Jerusalem community, is a representative of the mission to the Jews, while Paul and Barnabas, major leaders of the Antioch community (at the time of the council), are representatives of the mission to the Gentiles. Paul vigorously defends a "no circumcision" position and leaves with his leadership and message as not just being approved but as having the same authority as that of the apostles. He held that to submit oneself to circumcision indicated that one was willing to live one's life according to the Mosaic Law which is no longer necessary because of the revelation made through Jesus the Christ. *For Further Study:* See JMc, "ACTS OF THE APOSTLES"—3rd and 4th paragraphs, p. 11; "CEPHAS"; and "CIRCUMCISION." Read WB and AC 2:1—2:21.

3RD WEEK: READ GALATIANS 3:1—3:29. (Gal. 3:19-29; also see Rom. 3:20, 5:13, and 7:7-8) Why *did* God give the law to His chosen people? How does the law relate to faith? How do you personally see salvation and how do you receive it? What light has this chapter shed on the following areas of your life: faith, law, tradition, works, responsibility, loyalty?

Resource Material/Indicators: For Paul a person is made righteous by God through the gift of faith, not by the adherence to religious laws or the performance of good works. Faith, here, refers to the complete committing of one's entire person in response to the loving, accepting, forgiving Father that one personally experiences in Jesus the Christ. Paul demonstrates these points by having the Galatians reflect on their own religious encounters with God and by telling a story of Abraham, a person who lived prior to the existence of the Mosaic law but who was righteous because of his faith. Two of the major points of this story which was created to deal with this problem of the law by Paul or those participating in the Gentile mission are that Abraham's true descendents are those who (a) believe in the Christ, and (b) believe that the promises God made before the Mosaic law was created are not now subject to these laws. The law can guide a person's actions and indicate his failures but cannot give life. Through faith all people—Jew or Gentile, male or female—participate in the fruits of the promises made to Abraham; and since we have an intimate relationship with God through Jesus Christ, all differences have lost their ultimate value. *For Further Study:* See JMc, "FAITH"—III. Paul; "LAW"—6. *Law and Covenant,* and 7. *The Torah in Judaism;* and II. The Pauline Writings. Read WB and ACTS 3:1—3:29.

4TH WEEK: READ GALATIANS 4:1 —4:31. (Gal. 4:6-7) What does it mean to you to be able to call God "Abba! Father!"? (Gal. 4:28) What does it mean to you to be a child of God's promise?

Resource Material/Indicators: Paul continues to defend his position by further reinterpreting Abraham's experience in light of the understanding of salvation given by Jesus' death and resurrection. Not by one's blood line or performance of religious actions is one saved but by God's totally free giving of the Spirit who is not a reward but a loving gift. (See Rom. 8:14-17). Jesus' Spirit, now living and active in one's person and life, causes a new perspective of and relationship to God and other people. This results in changing one's priorities, values, attitudes, and life style. The Christian is asked by Jesus to personally address God as "Abba" (Daddy). In the tale of Sarah (Gen. 21:2-5) and Hagar (Gen. 16:1-16), Paul states that the fruits of God's promise to Abraham do not depend on a physical birth but on a spiritual one. While Hagar and Ishmael symbolize the old Jerusalem and Jewish nation which were founded in and hindered by the Sinai covenant, Sarah and Isaac represent the new Jerusalem and Christians which are founded in and freed by Jesus Christ in whom the promises (Gen. 17:16-21) made to Abraham are fulfilled. *For Further Study:* See JMc, "ABBA" and "ABRAHAM"—4. *The Religion of Abraham,* and 5. *Abraham in later Scriptures.* Read WB and ACTS 4:1—4:31.

5TH WEEK: READ GALATIANS 5:1 —5:26. (Gal. 5:1-3) Why do you think Paul was so adamant with the Galatians on circumcision in view of Luke's account in Acts 16:1-3? Why does Paul refer to the cross as a "scandal" and at the same time as a source of freedom?

Resource Material/Indicators: Paul speaks of a God who is close to his creation and who continuously seeks out all people and meets and frees them in Jesus' ministry, death and resurrection. God neither holds one's failures and weaknesses against him nor requires that one become something he cannot, but accepts and forgives all as they are. This Father frees us from a life which demands that our actions make us both good and worthy of His love. The cross is a scandal because it is a paradoxical symbol showing how we cannot achieve salvation on our own, with our powerlessness and helplessness; we also need God's infinite love and forgiveness which empower us to love. This liberation is not self-centered but other-centered, i.e., to be totally at the disposition of others. The Spirit which founds and lives in the Christian community initiates loving actions. The fruits of the Spirit mentioned in Galatians 5:22 are a sign of the true Spirit's presence, while the list of vices given in 5:19-20 are typical pagan vices. For Paul there is no compromise; either one is for the Law or for Christ. *For Further Study:* JMc, "CROSS", 2nd paragraph, p. 162; and "SPIRIT"— III. *Paul.* Read WB and ACTS 5:1—5:26.

6TH WEEK: READ GALATIANS 6:1—6:18. In what ways can you "fulfill the law of Christ" (6:2)? What are the main points that Paul has conveyed in his letter to the Galatians? How can these lessons be applied today?

Resource Material/Indicators: The Christian lives the law of Christ—a law of love which is not confined to a particular set of rules or format but is expressed in any way which is truly beneficial to others. The one who, in faith, takes up his/her responsibility for his/her neighbor is given eternal life which here refers to the Kingdom of God. Here, to give a final impact to his arguments, in concluding Paul contrasts what he can boast about with that of the Judaizers. Paul is not concerned about people thinking that he is insane for preaching a paradoxical message or that he would not find favor with other people. He relies upon and has found favor with the Father. Paul's own suffering and physical scars do not represent personal gain but the glory of Christ. The Greek word used here which is translated as "marks" was ordinarily used to indicate the mark of ownership burned on an animal or slave. Jesus' Spirit, not the law, is in the hearts of Christians, transforming and challenging them to become more than they are at the present—a new creation! *For Further Study:* Read WB and *ACTS 6:1—6:18.*

Originally published by *Catholic Charismatic* compiled by Chuck Piazza, Jane Caccamo and Clarence Roberts